DRAMATIC HISTORY OF INDIA

—29 PLAYLETS—

THE DELHI DURBAR OF 1911.

By kind permission of the Trustees, Victoria Memorial Section, Indian Museum.

DRAMATIC HISTORY OF INDIA

—29 PLAYLETS—

FLORA ANNIE STEEL

THIRD EDITION

GYAN

Published by

Gyan Publishing House
5, Ansari Road
Daryaganj, New Delhi-110002
Phone: 011-47034999, 9811692060
E-mail: books@gyanbooks.com

Distribution Network
gyanbooks.com
India, USA, Canada, UK, Australia, France

ISBN : 9788121233316 (PB)
First Published, Bombay

2nd Impression 2020

Printed at: Gyan Press, Delhi.

Dramatic History of India
–29 Playlets–
Author: Flora Annie Steel

DRAMATIC HISTORY OF INDIA

—29 PLAYLETS—

FLORA ANNIE STEEL

AUTHOR OF "TALES FROM THE PANJAB," "INDIA THROUGH THE AGES," ETC., ETC.

THIRD EDITION

BOMBAY

K. & J. COOPER

EDUCATIONAL PUBLISHERS

CONTENTS.

DRAMATIC HISTORY OF INDIA.

—1—

THE PROMISED LAND.

The Aryans came down to India in the beginning of Time from the highlands of Upper Asia. They came through the Punjab. They brought with them their flocks and herds. In the Rig-Veda we have a collection of their hymns, and it gives us also a few facts regarding their lives and their beliefs; also it speaks of what they found in India. The cause of their migration is not known. One hymn says it was because the seasons in the high uplands changed, and there was ten months' winter and two months of summer. You can trace the wanderings of the Aryan race by the Aryan words in various languages. *Duhitar* is one of these. It is *daughter* in English, *tochter* in German. It means a milkmaid.

DRAMATIS PERSONÆ.

A RISHI. A MILKMAID. 1ST SHEPHERD.
A RUNNER. 2ND SHEPHERD.

SCENE.

The end of a mountain pass. THE RISHI (*an old white-bearded blind man*) *seated on a projecting rock which overlooks the plains of India below. Beside him stands a maiden* (THE MILKMAID) *carrying a pot brimful of milk.*

RISHI. Would I have my vanished sight once more! Tell me, daughterling, how looks this promised land towards which we have been journeying these months and years?

MILKMAID. [*Setting down her pot of milk and shading her eyes with her hand.*] It seems to have no end, grandad! Further and yet further it stretches till the purple edge of it is lost in the purple mists.

RISHI. Canst see water, daughterling?—water for the flocks and herds.

MILKMAID. There be five silver snakes curving southward through the land; they must be rivers.

RISHI. Good! And the land looks fair and rich?

MILKMAID. Ay! there should be pasturage enough and to spare for our flocks and herds. They will forget their long wanderings from the Roof-of-the-World. [*Wistfully.*] But who can ever forget the upland meadows they have left, where the spring flowers!

RISHI. True, my daughter, they were beautiful; but the snow lay too long, the summer was all too short. So the word came to wander. [*Restlessly.*] Sure it is time news came of the advance party. They promised to send back to say how they fared.

MILKMAID. [*Looking intently.*] Methought I saw something on the upward path. Yes! it is a man running. The news comes, grandad!

RISHI. Now Agni and all the gods send it be good news!

[*Enter the* RUNNER *who falls at the* RISHI'S *feet and touches them with his forehead.*]

RUNNER. Hail, wisest of the wise! I bring good news. Our party hath advanced many miles into the promised land, and found it even more than they expected. They have vanquished the enemy.

RISHI. Then it is an inhabited land?

RUNNER. Inhabited. [*He squats down, and turns to the* MILKMAID.] Lo! sister, if I have to tell all I have seen, I require breath; and my mouth is dry. Prithee, a draught from thy milk-pot. [*She gives it. He takes a long pull and commences. During this time, the* SHEPHERDS *have come in and stand listening.*] Know, O most wise! the land is full of peoples; but not all one kind. There be two; the black and the red. The black are Dasyus, or robbers. They have no noses.

1ST SHEPHERD. Say you so? Wah! Wah!

2ND SHEPHERD. Wah! Wah! Say you so?

[*They stroke their own straight noses affectionately.*]

RUNNER. Not that they have not nostrils set as it were in a button; but they have no nose to speak of. [*He strokes his own affectionately.*]

2ND SHEPHERD. Say you so? Wah! Wah!

1ST SHEPHERD. Wah! Wah! Say you so?

RISHI. Enough of noses! What language do these people speak?

RUNNER. Most wise! they utter fearful yells. But they shoot well with bows and arrows. Still we prevail and drive them from their woods and forests.

RISHI. That is well! After these long nights of wanderings the dawn comes at last. Praise be to thee Ushas, shining-robed Maiden of Light! And what of the red people?

RUNNER. They be of a different kidney; not so easy of conquest. They have iron cities.

RISHI. Iron!

RUNNER. Ay, most wise! And they till the ground with iron ploughs and sow seeds so that their flocks may feed.

1ST SHEPHERD. Wah! Wah! Say you so?

2ND SHEPHERD. Say you so? Wah! Wah!

RISHI. So can we learn to do if need be. Go on, Runner.

RUNNER. And they have temples; not the open sky as we have, but carven buildings.

RISHI. [*Quickly.*] And their rites are doubtless different from ours. They are accursed.

RUNNER. And they are rich beyond compare. Their women —

MILKMAID. [*Eagerly.*] Then there be women?

RUNNER. Many, my sister, and most beautiful; all covered with gold and jewels!

[*The two* SHEPHERDS *and the* MILKMAID *give a sigh of content.*]

RISHI. [*Rising.*] It is enough! [*He stretches his hand out over the distance he cannot see.*] Yea! my children, the news is good. We have travelled far hoping always for this day. It has come at last; and though my outward eyes be sightless, with my inward ones I see a day far off in the years when the flood of my people shall have filled this promised land. So here, O Milkmaid! let us pour a libation to the gods, and sing the sacred hymn of the sacred Soma — the drink that makes men as the gods.

[*The* MILKMAID *pours milk upon the ground; they stand with uplifted hands and chant the sacred hymn.*]

CHANT.

Soma! born of the mountains, succulent, golden,
Sweet-smelling plant and fair growing, all worship be thine
In the draught of thy healing are hidden and holden
The things men desire and covet to make them divine.
Plucked in the moonlight, and pressed with right charmings,
Free us from sorrow and grief, from fear and alarmings.
Forward and straight let us go, inspired by Soma,
Forward as deed-doers ever, the followers of Soma.

—2—

THE MAHABHARATA.

This is the great epic of India. So well known is it to the Indian people that its words and its wisdom are part and parcel of their daily life. It is not historical, but it is the only record we have of the time which came after the Vedic or Aryan times. Most people see in it only an account of a war that is supposed to have raged between two tribes called the Kauravas and the Pandavas; but it is more than that. It is amongst other things the story of a splendid knight-errant by name Bhishma, or 'The Terrible': a knight who takes worthy place beside those of the Round Table, for justice, honour, and bravery, and of whom every Indian boy should be proud.

DRAMATIS PERSONÆ.

BHISHMA, a hero.
ARJUNA, the third Pandava Prince.
YUDHISHTHIRA, the eldest Pandava Prince.
BHIMA, the second Pandava Prince.
DURYODHANA, the eldest Kaurava Prince.
KARNA, a young noble attached to the Kauravas.
DRONA, their Master of Arms.

SCENE I.

A Garden. In one of the alleys a target has been set up, and a crowd of boys, laughing and shouting, are shooting at it with bows and arrows. The boys are all first cousins, being the five Pandava princes, sons of the dead king Pandu, and the hundred sons of his brother, the blind king Dhritarashtra. Bhishma, their great-uncle and tutor, a tall handsome man with a grave face and hair streaked with grey, sits watching the boys from the steps of a summer-house.

YUDHISHTHIRA. Now is Arjuna's turn.

DURYODHANA. [*Sneering.*] Arjuna! always Arjuna! One would think the world held no skill but his. Karna can beat him at single-stick any day. Canst thou not, Karna?

KARNA. [*Setting his lips.*] We shall see, never fear. I challenge him. I challenge him.

BHIMA. [*With a loud guffaw, stretching his huge muscular arms.*] And me at wrestling, mayhap? But look you, cousin, I back Arjuna to shoot or do anything else against the whole lot of you Kauravas: so there!

DURYODHANA. [*Fiercely.*] Do you? Hark to what the bull-necked beast saith, boys! Shall he insult us?

BOYS. No! No! [*They gather round.*]

BHISHMA. [*Calling.*] Boys! boys! remember you play a game. If it be Arjuna's turn let him have it. To be just is to be as the gods.

[*The tumult subsides.* ARJUNA *shoots and the arrow quivers in the very centre of the mark.*]

ALL THE BOYS. Wah! Wah! Well done! well done!

ARJUNA. Stop a bit. I can beat that, I think.

[*He draws again and the second arrow hits and splits the first.*]

ALL THE BOYS. Wah! Wah! Arjuna is indeed the victor. Well done! well done!

[ARJUNA *delighted at his success, throws aside his bow, and runs to* BHISHMA *for sympathy. He climbs on* BHISHMA'S *knee and flings his arms round his neck.*]

ARJUNA. Didst see ?. I did it! I did just as thou and Master Drona did teach me, O my father!

BHISHMA. [*Rises and sets down the boy quietly.*] I am not thy father, O Bharata!

[ARJUNA *watches him surprised as he walks away, then turns to the* MASTER OF ARMS.]

ARJUNA. Wherefore did he say that so sadly? And whose son am I, if not his? We all call him grandsire.

[THE BOYS *gather round.*]

DRONA. Ye be all sons of kings.

YUDHISHTHIRA. Ay! but their father [*he points to the Kaurava princes*] is blind, and blind men are not kings by right.

DRONA. Have a care, young sir. What you spit at the sky falls on your face. Thy father, so they say, was a white leper: but both through no fault, but by heaven's chance. It is a goodly story.

ALL THE BOYS. Tell it us.

DRONA. Well, the game being over, it might cool your minds and bodies; and knowledge prevents folk from quarrelling like quails in a cage. Well, see you, my Lord Bhishma was his father's only son and heir to the throne. But, so dearly did he love and honour his father, that to enable him to marry a beautiful girl he loved, my Lord Bhishma took an oath never to marry, and never to claim the throne.

That was to belong to his father's son by the beautiful girl. And all these years, my Lord Bhishma has kept his oath, though many a fair damsel has wanted him. All the three maidens he brought from far to be brides for his half-brother, the King, wanted him, but he held fast to his oath. One went away and died of grief. Your grandmother, O Kauravas! wanted him too. She refused to look at the husband they brought her, and wept so much that her son—your father—was born blind. And your grandmother, O Pandavas! for desire of him, looked at the husband they brought her with such loathing and turned so pale with fear that your father was born a white leper. But to all my Lord Bhishma gave the same reply: "I will renounce the three worlds, and all that may be greater than these, but my oath will I not renounce." And all these years hath he been guardian of the King and the princes, and the land and all have flourished. Lo! the wheel of virtue having been set in motion by my Lord Bhishma, all are brave, learned, honest and happy. It is a golden age!

[THE BOYS *sit thoughtful, till* BHISHMA *returning from his walk aside rallies them.*]

BHISHMA. What! all silent and glum. Youth should have no cares, and brave men need but to fight their best and let victory or defeat come as please the gods. But, mark you, boys, they must fight with honour. Remember the rule: "With one who has thrown away his sword, with one fallen, with one flying for his life, with one yielding, with woman, or one bearing the name of woman, or with low, vulgar fellows no gentleman ever fights." Come, say it after me, boys, lest you forget.

[BOYS *repeat after him, chanting.*]

" With one who hath thrown away his sword,
With one flying for his life,
With one fallen, with one yielding,
With woman, or one with woman's name,
With low or vulgar fellows I do no battle."

BHISHMA. Boys, dear to me all as sons, that is the true soldier's rule. So now to games once more. Karna hath challenged the Pandava to single-stick.

ALL THE BOYS. Hurrah ! Hurrah !

DRAMATIS PERSONÆ.

KING DHRITARASHTRA, the blind king.

YUDHISHTHIRA, the Pandava Prince lately appointed heir-apparent.

DURYODHANA, the disappointed Kaurava Prince.

DRAUPADI, wife to Yudhishthira.

SHAKUNI, King of Gandhara, and maternal uncle of the Kaurava Princes ; an expert gambler ; uses loaded dice ; desires Draupadi.

BHIMA, brother to Yudhishthira.

VIDURA, a wise counsellor
BHISHMA, the Grandsire } desirous of peace.
DRONA, the Preceptor

Nobles, Pandava and Kaurava Princes, etc., etc.

SCENE II.

A crystal arched Hall. It has a thousand pillars each inlaid with gold and lapis lazuli. The floor is covered with many-hued carpets, bordered in gold. It is filled with a splendid assemblage of kings and princes seated separately or in pairs on costly seats of beautiful shape and colour. In a centre is the gaming table with dice ready on it.

BHISHMA. Hearken! O my children. Let not strife come between you. The Kauravas and the Pandavas are brothers, have been brothers since boyhood, should be brothers till death.

DURYODHANA. [*Sneering.*] Brothers, O Grandsire, should have equal rights; yet Yudhishthira hath the heirship to the kingdom.

VIDURA. [*Sternly.*] Because he is of all most wise, most patient, most just. Such choice is of the gods; so cease from jealousy, Duryodhana. And thou, O Yudhishthira? bethink thee. Gambling is unfair. Remember thou wilt be king.

YUDHISHTHIRA. I do remember it, most wise. For that reason I accept my cousin's challenge. No monarch can do less.

SHAKUNI. [*Impatiently.*] The assembly is set, and I, Prince Duryodhana's proxy, am prepared. I prithee begin — unless thou art afraid.

YUDHISHTHIRA. [*Seizing the dice box.*] Not I. See here, O cousin! This fair string of pearls won from the ocean, is my first stake; — and yours?

DURYODHANA. This row of priceless emeralds.

SHAKUNI. Done! [*They throw.*] Good fortune waits on me. See! I have won.

YUDHISHTHIRA. [*Beginning to wax warm.*] Not so fast, my friend! I stake the money in my treasury; — and you?

DURYODHANA. [*Contemptuously.*] The same, and with thy pearls thrown in.

[*They throw,* SHAKUNI *with his loaded dice wins.*]

YUDHISHTHIRA. [*Becoming visibly excited.*] I stake my armies and my serving-men.

DURYODHANA. The same, with all that thou hast lost, thrown in.

[*They go on staking and throwing until* YUDHISHTHIRA, *ruined, sans money, sans kingdom, sans men, covers his face with his hands.*]

BHISHMA. [*With emotion.*] Honour remains, my son. With that a brave man counts himself a king. Thou art thyself, remember.

DURYODHANA. [*Evilly.*] He hath himself to stake if he wills it. What say you, Yudhishthira? Thyself as king?

YUDHISHTHIRA. [*Wildly.*] If all else is lost. why not myself? Yea! I accept.

[*They throw.* SHAKUNI *wins.*]

VIDURA. [*Protesting.*] Ah! Duryodhana, naught is gained by this. Wealth, kingdoms, power are nothing. These men will soon regain what they have lost: for they are heroes. Win them to thy side by love and kindness. They will be more to you than all the wealth they have.

DURYODHANA. [*With a laugh.*] A good idea. Come, my cousin, you have something left to stake — your brothers.

YUDHISHTHIRA. My brothers? Never!

BHIMA. Bethink thee, brother! Thou hast given thyself as king to these gross robbers. Give us at least the chance of rescue. Done, Shakuni, done! Ourselves 'gainst all that he has lost.

[*They throw and lose. The vast assembly is divided between pleasure and pain : some favouring the Kauravas, some the Pandavas.*]

DURYODHANA. [*Rubbing his hands.*] That clinches it.

YUDHISHTHIRA. [*In utter despondence.*] That clinches it. Brother, forgive me.

SHAKUNI. [*Leaning over and whispering to* YUDHISHTHIRA.] All is not lost ! Thy Queen remains — fair Draupadi.

YUDHISHTHIRA. [*Starting up.*] My Queen ? Never ! He bids me stake my Queen, my wife.

[*The assembly thrills. Faint cries of " Shame ! shame ! "*]

BHISHMA. [*In a broken voice.*] Oh, son most wise, forbear !

VIDURA. This is rank infamy.

DRONA. Send thy steel through his heart; thou knowest the way !

YUDHISHTHIRA. [*Slowly.*] Yet if by her I won my brothers back, if by her aid these robbers were undone, would she not welcome it ? Ay ! Draupadi against the world ? I'll back her to the last drop of my blood.

[*The assembly rings with cries of " Forbear, forbear." Every man hangs on the verdict as* SHAKUNI *rattles the dice. Then utter silence reigns as* SHAKUNI *says in a shaking voice, " Fair Draupadi is ours ! "* YUDHISHTHIRA *sinks back overcome with shame, grief, and remorse.* DURYODHANA *laughs cruelly.* SHAKUNI *puts aside the dice box with trembling hands.*]

DURYODHANA. We have won the Queen, and now will take our prize. Bid her come hither, Chamberlain.

YUDHISHTHIRA. [*Feebly.*] Not here, before these all.

DURYODHANA. She is won by dice, therefore a slave; and slaves cannot object.

CHAMBERLAIN. [*Returning.*] The Queen refuses to obey, but sends this message to her lord: "Who was thy master when thou lost me at the dice, thyself or someone else?"

[YUDHISHTHIRA *is too prostrate to reply.*]

DURYODHANA. [*Angrily.*] Bring her hither! If she come not peaceably, by force.

[*Murmurs of shocked surprise and dissent from the assembly. Enter* DRAUPADI, *dragged in by guards*]

DRAUPADI. [*Indignant.*] Shame on ye all to drag me here, a queen, like any slave! But here, before ye all, I ask my lord this question — only one: "Wert thou free man when thou didst stake thy wife, or hadst thou lost thyself and so become a slave? [DURYODHANA *looks hurriedly at* SHAKUNI *and* SHAKUNI *at* DURYODHANA.] For, if thou wert a slave how didst thou dare, being slave, to stake a free woman on the hazard of the die?" My lords! my lords! this is unheard-of infamy. I claim the right of freedom. I, the Queen, cannot be bought or sold by any slave. Ah Duryodhana! thou'rt too cunning to be wise. I and the Pandava princes have escaped thee.

[*The assembly carried away by her words breaks into applause and assent.*]

DHRITARASHTRA. [*Rising from his throne.*] Oh! first of all the daughters my sons have brought to me, most wise, most virtuous, thou art right. No slave can barter a free woman. Thou art free, and free to ask of me what favour thou desirest as reward.

DRAUPADI. The favour that my son may never say, "My father was a slave." Set Yudhishthira free, O King!

DHRITARASHTRA. Lo! he is free.

DURYODHANA. I claim my right of chance. Once more the dice shall say whether we princes of the Kaurava race, go into exile for a dozen years, or they of Pandu's blood. Shakuni! the dice.

BHISHMA. [*Imploring.*] No, not again! Evil will come from this and quarrels without end. I bid you all beware!

YUDHISHTHIRA. Grandsire! let be, my honour is at stake. I'll take no favour from these miscreants.

[*He throws and loses.*]

Come, my brothers! come my Queen. We go, but we go fighting to the end. Ay, and the fight will last until we win.

[*Exeunt to martial music.*]

DRAMATIS PERSONÆ.

BHISHMA, the Grandsire.
ARJUNA, a Pandava Prince.
YUDHISHTHIRA, a Pandava Prince.
SHIKHANDIN, a Prince.
DRONA, the Preceptor.
BHIMA and the twin-brothers, NAKULA and SAHADEVA, Pandava Princes.
Nobles, Soldiers, etc.

SCENE III.

A wide plain, mostly sand. Heavy clouds, storms of rain, thunder, lightning.

[BHISHMA *and* DRONA *enter followed by their escort.*]

BHISHMA. Time passes and the conflict that began twelve years ago with Prince Shakuni's loaded dice will never end until I die. Yet death is not for me because the tie of duty to the Kaurava race binds me to life. Yet my heart is sad. I would not war against the Pandava heroes. Are they not my sons as well as the Kauravas?

DRONA. Most true, O mighty one! My skill it was that strung Arjuna's bow. Well! the die is cast. We must fight on, as brave men fight for duty, for our cause. [*Exeunt all.*]

[*Enter* ARJUNA *and* YUDHISHTHIRA *followed by* SOLDIERS.]

ARJUNA. But for the words the Holy One spoke even now, I could not war against our Grandsire. Think how good he was of old. How well he fathered us poor fatherless boys. Yet as the Great One said: "Life is not slain, Life cannot slay: the Spirit lasts for ever." So let us on.

YUDHISHTHIRA. Nay! I must seek for counsel ere I fight.

[*Exeunt all.*]

[*Re-enter* BHISHMA, SOLDIERS *and a* HERALD. *They seat themselves.*]

BHISHMA. Let us rest ourselves and seek good counsel of the gods.

HERALD. My Lord Yudhishthira craves an audience of great Bhishma.

BHISHMA. Let him come.

[*Enter* YUDHISHTHIRA.]

YUDHISHTHIRA. I come a suppliant on the eve of war to beg thy blessing, Grandsire, and thy leave, to battle with the best, the bravest of all men — thyself, whom all revere and love!

BHISHMA. Thou hast it, O my son!

Bound am I to the Kurus by my salt,
But thee do I love also. Blest indeed
Art thou for coming thus. Hadst thou forgot,
I must have cursed thee. Now,
Battle excepted, what dost thou desire?

YUDHISHTHIRA. Wisest of men! none dare to ask of thee aught but fidelity. Yet if we slay thee not, defeat is ours. How shall we compass victory?

BHISHMA. None of the race of men can vanquish me, and for my death —

That only comes to me of my free will.
But fight on bravely, gain the victory
And bid Arjuna keep his arrows sharp.
Thou hast my blessing. Now I must go hence.

[*Exeunt different ways.*]

[*Noise of fighting.* SOLDIERS *run on and off. Loud cries, clashing of swords and spears.*]

ARJUNA. [*Running on breathless, followed by* SHIKHANDIN, YUDHISHTHIRA *and* SOLDIERS.] Foiled again! There's something in his eye that makes me quail. I think how oft I've sat upon his kindly knee. Ah, Bhishma! Bhishma! Fate is hard indeed.

[*Runs off fighting.*]

YUDHISHTHIRA. Yet if Grandsire lives, we Pandavas are undone. 'Gainst him we cannot win.

SHIKHANDIN. Most true, my prince! and yet — Thou knowest my story: how my mother hid even from my father that she had borne a boy, and brought me up a girl. She was the Princess Amba, and had a grudge against great Bhishma in the past. He bore her off and would not marry her. He had some oath of celibacy. Then when I grew to man's estate she changed my name to Shikhandin from Shikhandini, sent me forth a warrior, and here I am ready to do my part. Great Bhishma oft has said, "With womankind, or one who bears or who has borne their name I do no battle." Let me try my luck.

YUDHISHTHIRA. [*Thoughtfully.*] I like it not; and yet, the battle must be won. Hark! here they come again. Go thou and help.

[*Noise of fighting as before. Exit* SHIKHANDIN.]

[*Exit* YUDHISHTHIRA: *re-enter* BHISHMA *breathless.*]

BHISHMA. Halt! I will rest awhile. Arjuna's shafts strike home. Ha! who come here, unarmoured and alone? Yudhishthira, Bhima, Arjuna and the twins. Welcome, my sons, a thousand welcomes! Wherefore do ye come?

YUDHISHTHIRA. To ask thy guidance, wisest of all men! how in this battle we shall conquer thee. Without it we are lost!

BHISHMA. Oh! ye my sons, my blessing on you rest, that you do seek such counsel. Yet have I none to give save this. Remember when you think of me the rule I gave you when as yet ye were but boys.

With one who hath thrown away his sword,
With one flying for his life,
With one fallen, with one yielding,
With woman or one with woman's name
I do no battle.

Yea! I will bare my bosom to the shaft of such as these. That is my answer. Farewell! I go to fight. [*Exit.*]

[*The five brothers bow their heads silently and go out.*]

HERALD. To arms! to arms! The enemy is nigh.

[*Again confused sounds of fighting.* SOLDIERS *pass and repass.*]

[*Enter* ARJUNA *and* SHIKHANDIN.]

ARJUNA. There is no way but this. Go thou before me without fear, O Shikhandin! Great Bhishma will not strike thee.

SHIKHANDIN. My sword is sharp. I will avenge my mother!

[*Exeunt.*]

[*Fighting is heard behind the scenes.*]

BHISHMA'S VOICE. These arrows cutting like the cold of winter, they are not Shikhandin's. They pierce me to the very heart, for they are Arjuna's. Yet Shikhandin stands there before me and I will not strike. 'Gainst women and 'gainst those who bear their names, I do no battle.

[*Cries from behind scenes.*]

CRIES. Bhishma falls! Bhishma has fallen!

BHISHMA'S VOICE. [*Faint yet distinct.*]

Yea! I have fallen pierced by many shafts.
And yet I die not till the sun shall rise
From its declension to the brave ascent
Towards highest light. I will lie here
Upon my bed of arrows and the world shall learn
From me the secret that has kept me pure.
A spirit cannot die—it lives for ever!

[*Slow music.*]

—3—

THE PARRICIDES.

The Saisunaga kings lived on the outside edge of reliable Indian history. The line began about 600 B. C. At first their capital was Rajagriha. Afterwards it was removed to Pataliputra, which was built by Ajatasatru. Very little is known of the Saisunagas save that their reigns were contemporaneous with the lives of two of the greatest men who ever lived, Gautama Buddha and Mahavira the founder of the Jain religion. Of Ajatasatru this is known that he killed his father; legend says by starvation. It also asserts that the four kings after him followed his example and became parricides.

DRAMATIS PERSONÆ.

AJATASATRU, King of Magadha.
DEVADATTA, the Buddha's first cousin and bitterest enemy.
DARSAKA, the king's son aged four.
A CHAMBERLAIN.
A WANDERING MENDICANT.

SCENE.

A Palace. The remains of a feast set in the wide hall. A low couch on which reclines a man; an older man with a cunning face is seated on the carpet beside him. It is night.

DEVADATTA. My lord the King seems of low spirits to-night. Wherefore? Has not all gone well? The kingdom of Kosala is subdued. Even the mighty Persian Darius has checked his victorious march, before touching Your Majesty's territories. And round this fort, built at the junction of the rivers, will grow in time a town unrivalled throughout all India for magnificence: a town far finer than New Rajagriha which your father built.

AJATASATRU. [*Turning pale and starting.*] My father! Mention him not, O Devadatta! Even to-day in all the mirth and revelry that rang through these walls—because I, Ajatasatru, had overcome all mine enemies—I seemed to hear those groans that drove me from Rajagriha, Rajagriha that he built.

DEVADATTA. My lord! be calm; the prize is worth the price.

AJATASATRU. [*Wildly.*] Worth it? Oh! curses on your lying tongue. Is it worth it to see as I do, if I take a moment's thought, the old man in his dungeon dying slowly, dying of starvation?

DEVADATTA. I say that it is worth it. You were born to rule and make your subjects happy. Were you not the King, where were they?

AJATASATRU. [*More calmly.*] There is *that* in it, no doubt. And the old man was past his prime. He could not have gained what I have gained, or ruled as I have ruled. And so I told the Blessed Buddha when I confessed my sin to him. I said, "Sin has overcome me, Lord, weak and foolish and wrong that I am, in that for the sake of sovereignty, I killed my father." And the Blessed One granted me pardon.

DEVADATTA. [*With an evil smile.*] If Buddha's pardon comfort my lord, so be it! This slave does not need such poor stuff. He contents himself with realities — such as this!

[CHAMBERLAIN *enters leading the King's little son, a fine boy of four, who leaps to the King's breast.*]

DARSAKA. I have come to say good-night, father.

AJATASATRU. [*Fondly.*] Eye of my heart's core, of my inmost soul! you would not sleep well, without your father's blessing, would you? [*They embrace.*]

CHAMBERLAIN. [*Returning.*] An aged mendicant is at the door.

AJATASATRU. Give him alms.

MENDICANT. [*Pushing aside the* CHAMBERLAIN.] I need no alms. I would not touch one crumb that fell from your rich table, parricide! Long years ago, I saw your father thus. His son was in his arms as yours is now. He called down blessings on your head, and now, a wasted skeleton done to death by greed, he lies while you feast proudly in his place. Well! so be it. This fate that you have conjured into life, shall linger in your race. That little lad shall hunger for your life — ay! take it too. His son, your grandson, with the poison of your deed born in his veins, and his son too —

AJATASATRU. [*Wildly clasping his son.*] Enough! enough! On me may fall the punishment, but not on him! I tell you he is innocent.

MENDICANT. Yet must he die because you once forgot your duty to your father. Learn, O King! even the forgiveness of a righteous man — yea, even of the Buddha — cannot change the course of a crime. From age to age it bears its fruit until the harvest comes. So shall your race be called Parricides in this world's history. [*Exit, leaving the* KING *prostrate on the couch.*]

—4—

A GREAT CONQUEROR.

In 327 B. C. Alexander the Great invaded India. He crossed the Jhelum river, or, as he called it, the Hydaspes, and defeated the great army led by Porus. He then crossed the Chenab and came to the river Beas beyond which lay, by repute, a brave, well-equipped, more civilized foe than those he had already conquered. Here the spirit of his soldiers began to flag; they refused to go on. So the retreat began. Alexander, with bent head, re-passed the provinces through which he had passed like a flaming sword, and embarked, with all his troops, in boats on the river Jhelum, and after a libation to his gods and the great river Indus, whom he trusted to bring him to the sea, started for Macedonia. He died on the way back.

DRAMATIS PERSONÆ.

ALEXANDER THE GREAT, King of Macedon.
PORUS, an Indian King.
TAXILES, an Indian King.
MEROËS.
KOINOS, a Cavalry leader.

SCENE.

A BATTLE-FIELD.

ALEXANDER *is standing beside his chariot. Around him are officers of his staff. He has a roll of script in his hand and points with his finger to something inscribed on it.*

ALEXANDER. So far good! Dripping, half-drowned, my legions have yet prevailed so far in this the first great battle between East and West. By Jupiter! those two hundred leviathans of elephants couped up by the Macedonian cavalry, maddened with rage, was a sight to make a brave man tremble. Ye gods! but they fought well, those Indians, and their leader Porus. Ah! here comes Koinos from his arduous task. Well done! Koinos. Next to those who stole the passage of the river, your feat of leading two regiments of cavalry across the van of the enemy deserves reward. How goes it now?

KOINOS. They fight still, great Alexander. Foremost of them all fights brave Porus, their commander.

ALEXANDER. Ay! I saw him, a giant in stature, a lion for courage, holding at bay half-a-hundred of my picked soldiers. Such an enemy would make a good friend. See here, Taxiles, you are his comrade, of his race—or like to it. Go to him and take a message of peace. You can tell him, we Macedonians are fair in conquest as in fight.

TAXILES. [*Bowing.*] So have I found great Alexander. Since I yielded up the Serpent City willingly, I have still been king. I will take the message. [*Exit.*]

ALEXANDER. [*Musing.*] Yea! I would be friends with all these people if I could. But now to business. Bid the captains of the companies report; and Koinos, see you that the outposts are recalled. You, Meroës, look to your Indian contingent. I know not their ways; but in my army I will have no pillage. It is a brave foe we have defeated.

[*Re-enter* TAXILES *running.*]

TAXILES. 'Tis of no use, great Alexander! He is wounded in nine places and faint with thirst and loss of blood. But he fights still! Nay, when he saw me he turned and would have let loose a javelin at me but that I fled.

ALEXANDER. The more reason to save him. Go thou, Meroës, and shout at him from far my message of peace; then the brave fool must at least hear it.

MEROËS. I go, General. 'Twill not be my fault if he hears not. I can bellow like any bull.

[*Exit, bellowing.*]

ALEXANDER. [*Laughing.*] 'Tis well that we can laugh. By the gods, we are fortunate indeed! The odds were all against us — six to one. Yet not one hairbreadth of my plan has gone astray. I tell you, Koinos, in years to come, great generals will study my attack and find it good. [*Re-enter* MEROËS.]

MEROËS. I have won. He comes anon. I found him dismounted of his elephant half dead, yet propped against the beast, his sword still in his hand. Around him forty foes all thirsting for his blood. so I bade them desist and stood and bellowed. [*Coughs.*] Yea! I bellowed and I bellowed, till he could not choose but hear. And he comes amain. [*Stands and coughs.*]

ALEXANDER. [*Quickly.*] Charioteers make ready. I go to meet him. Bravery like this deserves all kingly honour.

[*He mounts his chariot and moves off slowly, followed by his staff. The stage is empty.*]

[*Enter* PORUS. *He is badly wounded but walks proudly, followed at a respectful distance by two Macedonians. He pauses and looks back at his guards.*]

PORUS. Not so close! Have I not given my word not to attempt escape? A brave man does not lie; and I am brave.

SOLDIERS. None brave, we dare swear.

PORUS. But what is bravery worth, if the great gods give not the brains to use it? This Greek General has fair out-witted me and I owe him homage for his cleverness: but not for courage or for bravery.

[*Enter* ALEXANDER *in his chariot followed by his staff. He descends.*]

ALEXANDER. By the gods, what a man! Mark you his stature and the brawny thews and sinews of his limbs. Look at his face, a veritable Mars. [*He advances and salutes* PORUS] Great King, great enemy, and greater warrior still, thy foe salutes thee. Speak! what dost thou require? Speak freely. Alexander listens.

PORUS. I would be treated in a kingly way.

ALEXANDER. Bravo! bravo! well said. So shall it be — for my sake, not thine own, since it is gain to treat a brave man bravely. But for thyself — I pray thee tell me what would be most pleasing to thee.

PORUS. Great General, thou knowest as well as I that Kingship holds all things, both small and great. I would be treated as a King — no more, no less.

ALEXANDER. Bravo again! Ah! Porus, thou sayest truth. Kingship should hold both victory and defeat, riches and poverty, yea! even joy and grief, as part and parcel of itself. So shall it be. I give thy country back its noble King. And to him also do I gift, for love of his great bravery and steadfastness, another country larger than his own. Clerk! see that the documents be duly writ. Porus! thy hand; foes once, in future, we are friends.

—5—

THE RIVALS.

DRAMATIS PERSONÆ.

CHANDRAGUPTA, King and Emperor.
CHANAKYA, his Prime Minister and devoted servant.
RAKSHASA, former Prime Minister of the Nandas.
A CLERK.
A CHAMBERLAIN.

SCENE.

At Pataliputra in the Palace. Constructed of timber it has gilded pillars wreathed with golden vines and set with silver birds. It stands in a wide garden studded with fish ponds and fountains and planted with a great variety of ornamental trees, shrubs and flowers. A wide hall opening to the garden contains a huge golden bath six feet in width, and on a richly carved table ewers and basins of pure gold are standing. Some of them are set with precious stones.

KING CHANDRAGUPTA *is reclining on a couch covered with rich gold tissue, and four female attendants are massaging him with ebony rollers.*

CLERK. [*Reading.*] By the orders of the Most Mighty, a horse and ox race will be held at the fourth watch.

CHANDRAGUPTA. Good, go on.

CLERK. [*Reading.*] The War Office reports as ready for service at the Most Mighty's command an army of

690,000, excluding followers. The admiralty has nothing to report. Transport Commissariat and Army Service, including drummers, grooms, mechanics and grass-cutters are all efficient and in order. Boards Nos. III, IV, V, VI, Infantry, Cavalry, War Chariots, Elephants are included in the War Office report.

CHANDRAGUPTA. [*Sleepily.*] Good, go on.

CLERK. [*Reading.*] The First Municipal Board hath settled the leather-workers' strike for wages, and one Bundranath hath been decapitated for causing the loss of an eye to an artizan of the first class.

CHANDRAGUPTA. Good. Not so hard, slave! not so hard. Send her away, toilet-master, and bring another.

[*The* MASSEUSE *goes weeping, another takes her place.*]

Go on, scribe.

CLERK. The Second Municipal Board hath decently buried a foreigner from China, administered his estate and is engaged in similar work with the many strangers in the capital. The Third Board hath prosecuted one Chrundas for failing to register the birth of his child within the appointed time, and one Govind for neglecting the death of his grandmother, such omissions being contrary to law and obstructive of the due levy of taxes.

CHANDRAGUPTA. Good, go on.

CLERK. The Fourth Board hath been busy inspecting the merchants' weights and measures, rectifying errors and duly stamping the royal stamp. A baker hath been fined and fifteen licences to trade are issued.

CHANDRAGUPTA. Good, go on. What hath the Fifth Board done?

CLERK. It hath supervised the merchandise and goods, separated new from old, thus aiding the Sixth Board which hath taken the tithe tax duly. The tax not having been evaded, no punishment by death has occurred.

CHANDRAGUPTA. [*Rising and dismissing attendants and clerk.*] So far good. My empire speeds on its way as steadfast as the stars. From the low pariah who sweeps the streets to the Most High, myself, all is in order, regulated, settled. Yet but a few short years ago I was a suppliant within the walls. This is Chanakya's work, my counsellor, my friend. I can fight well, my empire shows as much. From the Punjab to close upon the Eastern sea, from cold Himalaya to far Madura, it is all mine, and yet the veriest cur of a fat money-lender could outwit me clean. So 'tis Chanakya's doing that the late King's men are not in arms against me. Here he comes! Chanakya, thou art ever welcome.

[*They embrace.*]

CHANAKYA. And I feel welcome when I bring good news. And what I bring is good: 'tis somewhat of a story. Shall we sit? [*They sit.*]

Your Honour knows how often I have balked the schemes of those against you. A year ago you settled you would sleep in the pavilion. Going there one evening I noticed ants climb through a crevice in the wall, bearing the fragments of a recent meal. Instant I ordered that fire should be set to the pavilion for I guessed that murderers were hidden in some secret passage. Doubtless they were, since from that very day, some of the King's most noted foes have not been seen. [*Laughs.*] So with the poisoned draught I took and poured into a test goblet, then seeing the colour change, bade the physician drink. [*Laughs.*] Since when, O King, you choose fresh places to sleep in every night, and drink no drink save from a golden cup. Now to all this Rakshasa is the key. He was the late King's counsellor, as I am yours. To have him killed were easy; but it would have fanned rebellion into life. My end and aim have therefore been to gain him to our side. I have succeeded in it so far as this: he lives and is in our hands. His dearest friend awaits death on the scaffold. This must be our bribe to make him loyal. I have bidden the prison guards escort him hither and I hear them come. [*Rises.*]

CHANDRAGUPTA. Chanakya, your wisdom makes me cold. If you should turn against me!

CHANAKYA. Sooner the sun will turn from his ordered course! Here, my lord, is Rakshasa the Wise.

[*Enter* RAKSHASA.]

RAKSHASA. [*Aside.*] This must be the man, the vile Chanakya, rather let me own, the wise Chanakya, an exhaustless mine of learning, a deep ocean stored with gems. Let not my envy set aside his merits.

CHANAKYA. [*Smiling.*] So thou art Rakshasa whose enmity so long has held at bay and doomed to sleepless nights the King's best friends, and furnished me with themes of ceaseless thought. I am Chanakya, and I ask of you one question: Do you desire the life of Chandana, your dearest friend?

RAKSHASA. A needless question.

CHANAKYA. Ah! but what will say the King?

CHANDRAGUPTA. [*Smiling.*] What my preceptor says.

CHANAKYA. Nay! then 'tis easy. He cannot consent to grant such generous proof of grace while Rakshasa still holds aloof and wields the sword. But if he will assume [*Takes from his belt the Ministerial dagger.*] office in my place as Minister —

RAKSHASA. Pardon! I am not fit to bear what you so worthily have wielded.

CHANAKYA. [*Sternly.*] Lo? fitness and unfitness are as nothing! To be brief: the life of Chandana and your acceptance of ministerial office are conditions that cannot be disjoined. So you must choose.

[*A pause.*]

RAKSHASA. I yield me, Chandragupta. From this day I am your faithful servant.

CHANAKYA. [*Laughing and rubbing his hands.*] Wisdom hath won the day!

CHAMBERLAIN. [*To* CHANAKYA.] The executioners await the orders of Your Highness.

CHANAKYA. From Rakshasa must they take them now, since he directs the state and I —

CHANDRAGUPTA. Remain the guide, the counsellor, the friend.

CHANAKYA. Give my lord Rakshasa paper and pen. He would fain sign the pardon of his friend.

RAKSHASA. Chanakya, thou hast won indeed!

—6—

THE INDIAN CONSTANTINE.

The Emperor Asoka, the grandson of Chandragupta, who began to reign about 272 B.C., is rightfully given a place in the very front rank of the great kings not only of India, but of the whole world. Akbar was in some ways the better ruler, but Asoka saw deeper into the minds of the men he ruled. He began by being nick-named 'The Furious' on account of his vile temper; he ended as Piyadasi (Priyadarsin) 'The Humane.' This change was due to his conversion to Buddhism some twelve years after he came to the throne. From that time forth he employed his autocratic power in the teaching and enforcing of the Law of Piety. His missionaries went far afield, even to Europe; and before he died a vast proportion of the known world had been converted to Buddhism. Asoka's Law of Piety laid great stress on the rights of dumb animals as well as of men to just, fair, honourable treatment. He established hospitals for animals as well as for men throughout his dominions. The first hospital known to have been established in Europe was not founded till nearly one thousand years after Asoka's date. He always wore the yellow habit of a Buddhist monk.

DRAMATIS PERSONÆ.

ASOKA, Emperor of India.
A HERALD.
A MASTER OF THE HORSE.
A RICH MAN.
A POOR MAN.
Nobles, Men, Women, Children.

SCENE.

A ravine in the lower hills; an upright cliff of fine white quarts. A little way off, a royal tent stands and under the cliff a dais has been erected.

ASOKA. [*Standing alone on the dais, in a soft voice.*] O Herald! read the inscriptioh that all may hear, and hearing remember.

HERALD. Listen, ye people. This pious edict has been inscribed on living rock by His Sacred Majesty King Priyadarsin. [*Reads.*] Here must not animal be slaughtered even for sacrifice. Formerly even in the kitchen of King Priyadarsin, were thousands of animals slain daily. Now, but three are slain. Henceforward even these shall not be slaughtered. Everywhere throughout my dominions have hospitals been established — hospitals for men, hospitals for beasts; and healing herbs, medicinal for men and medicinal for beasts, have been planted. And the Law of Piety is this: Obedience to father and mother is good. Liberality to others is good, respect for the sacredness of life is good, avoidance of violence and extravagance is good. I have commanded that immediate report be made to me of all things at any hour and in any place. Hitherto I am not satisfied with my exertions or despatch of business. And work I must for the public benefit, and that I may discharge my debt of life, and make all animate beings in this world happy, so that they may gain heaven in the next. Hear, O people! nothing is of consequence save what concerns the next world, and the whole root of the matter is in exertion. [*Continues.*] Thus saith the King. This is inscribed in immutable rock for all time.

[*Plaudits from the crowd.*]

A VOICE. Heaven bless our beloved King!

ASOKA. Heaven preserve you, O my sons! Now if there be any here who hath a wrong to be righted let him come forward and state his case before me.

POOR MAN. [*Prostrating himself.*] O Merciful and Good! this rich man —

[*The* RICH MAN *steps forward superciliously. He holds by the bridle a richly caparisoned mule that shows evidence of a hard hasty ride.*]

bought of me that mule and agreed with me for twenty pieces of silver. He claimed a writing and had one made by his scribe. O Most Merciful! I cannot read and saw not that the figures were wrong, that instead of twenty but two were written. Now hath he taken the mule and given me but two pieces of silver. And Most Merciful, is that the price of so fair a mule?

ASOKA. [*Frowning, to* RICH MAN.] And what hast thou to say? How camest thou to buy this mule of that poor man for two pieces of silver?

RICH MAN. [*Volubly.*] Your Majesty is wise above all men! Your Majesty knows how some folk put extreme value on their possessions. This poor man had naught else, so he deems the mule of great value. But it hath a raw upon its back and for this reason he agreed with me, as it is written in the paper, for two pieces of silver. And he was quite content till news of Your Majesty's gracious coming reached him. Then without warning he decided to appeal causing me to ride hard many miles, day and night, in order to appear before Your Majesty.

ASOKA. [*Quietly.*] Master of the Horse, appraise the value of that mule roughly. Is it worth twenty pieces of silver or is it worth two?

MASTER OF THE HORSE. [*Looking over the mule.*] A mule that is worth two pieces of silver hath neither tail nor head, neither hath it legs — never saw I such a one. A mule that is worth twenty must have good paces, and such from the evidences of haste I would adjudge this one to have. If so ordered I will try it.

ASOKA. Enough! This mule hath four legs, a tail and a head. So much is evident. Therefore it is really worth more than two pieces of silver. But the writing remains — is it duly signed?

RICH MAN. [*Volubly, handing it up.*] Your Majesty will see all is in order.

ASOKA. It stands two pieces of silver sure enough. [*Folds up paper and returns it.*] The law adjudges in your favour without doubt; and yet — [*To* RICH MAN.] Couldst thou not spare yon poor man something more? The mule seems good.

RICH MAN. I am within the law.

ASOKA. Thou art indeed! [*To* POOR MAN.] Brother, I can do naught for thee save give advice — Go! Learn to read!

[*The* POOR MAN *salaams sorrowfully, the* RICH MAN *exultantly prepares to get on the mule.*]

[*In a voice of iron.*] Hold! Didst thou not say thy mule had a sore back! Go! Master of the Horse, unsaddle the poor beast and let me know the injury.

[*The* MASTER OF THE HORSE *obeys.*]

MASTER OF THE HORSE. The beast, Great King, hath signs of an old rub upon the withers long since healed, but from the haste with which it has been ridden recently, it hath a sore that will need treatment, nay that should, a day or two ago, have brought it rest.

ASOKA. [*To* RICH MAN.] Hearest thou what he says? Give thine excuse for riding this poor beast against the law which says all animals have equal rights with man to justice and fair treatment.

RICH MAN. [*Stuttering.*] My lord! My lord!

ASOKA. Bid the clerks fine him eighteen silver bits and give them of my grace to yon poor man who needs them sorely. Master of the Horse — the mule is confiscate. See that it goes to hospital and when recovered is sold by public auction. Farewell my friends! Remember! naught in this under-world can count against what will be in the world to come.

— 7 —

A HOUSE NOT MADE WITH HANDS.

When Asoka died, and the influence of his strong personality was no longer felt, his Empire broke up into petty independent states. From this date 232 B.C. to A.D. 320 when the Gupta line of kings began, India did not exist as a whole, and there is little to be set down as authentic. The following legend of St. Thomas the Christian apostle and King Gundaphar one of the Indo-Parthian kings is, however, very widespread.

Gundaphar, or Gondophares, as the Western writers call him, came to the throne of Parthia in A.D. 21. He thus forms a landmark in the otherwise somewhat dark ages.

DRAMATIS PERSONÆ.

ST. THOMAS, a Christian apostle.
HABBAN, a merchant.
AN OLD BRAHMAN.
AN OUTCASTE.
KING GUNDAPHAR.
HIS MINISTER.
Sick people, children, etc., etc.

SCENE.

A hospital. The patients are lying out on the verandah, and in the garden beyond. ST. THOMAS *is walking about attending to them.*

ST. THOMAS. [*Dropping a lotion into the* OLD BRAHMAN'S *eye.*] Thou wilt see clearer, brother, by and by. [*Passes to the* OUTCASTE *who is propped against a pillar.*] And thou, my son, [*He stoops to adjust a bandage on the man's foot.*] will be able to walk where thou choosest, yea! even into the palace of the King, by and by. One must have patience. God's mill grinds slowly but it grinds surely. [*He passes on to other sick folk.*]

HABBAN. He is a saintly man, for sure! Little thought I when I brought him overseas as a foreigner architect to build His Majesty King Gundaphar's new palace, that he was such a fellow. And yet it was strange how he came to me.

OLD BRAHMAN. How was't, brother?

HABBAN. See you, I had not drunk any wine being vowed to abstinence; but I had a vision. The Lord out of Heaven sold a man to me for twenty pieces of silver. Then next day I saw the very man in the market-place and he said, if I would give him twenty pieces of silver, he would come with me as architect to King Gundaphar. For I was seeking one. Now, whether I bought him or he bought me or the Lord out of Heaven bought us both, I know not. But this I do know, he is a saintly man.

OUTCASTE. Ay! none in the city but owe him something, though, mark you, he doth it all in the King's name. He feeds the hungry, he clothes the naked, he comforts the sorrowful, he succours the poor—all, mind you, in the King's name.

OLD BRAHMAN. Ay! the hospital is the King's hospital, the school the King's school. He must be a rich man to do it all.

HABBAN. He had nothing when he came aboard the ship with me save the twenty pieces of silver for which he sold himself.

OLD BRAHMAN. He gave that but yesterday as a festival for his school. See, here come the scholars.

[CHILDREN *troop in; each one, as they pass* ST. THOMAS *who stands to receive them, cries.*]

CHILDREN. Blessings on you, dear master! blessings on you.

ST. THOMAS. [*Smiling.*] Welcome, my pupils. Seat yourselves.

[CHILDREN *seat themselves in a half circle.*]

Now let us begin by singing of the golden palace not made with hands.

CHILDREN. [*Sing.*]

There's a golden palace
Built of loving deed,
Words that know no malice,
Thoughts that hold no greed.
Each of us can build it
Working at our best,
When with love we've filled it
There will take our rest.

There's a palace golden
Storm nor strife can harm —

MESSENGER. [*Running in.*] Peace! peace! Prepare yourselves. The King comes.

[CHILDREN *rise hurriedly.* SICK PEOPLE *crawl and crowd to the front. Cries of* "Heaven bless the King!" "Heaven bless our kindly King!" *rise on every side.*]

[ST. THOMAS *salutes smiling.*]

[*Enter* KING GUNDAPHAR *and his* MINISTER. *He stands surprised.*]

GUNDAPHAR. A welcome indeed, and a goodly sight in its way! But I came here for blame, not for praise. Minister, read the indictment to this gentleman.

MINISTER. [*Reading.*] "Whereas full six months ago, we, being satisfied you were a foreign architect, appointed you as chief architect to our realm, and bade you design and erect a palace for us that should have no peer upon this earth. And whereas ever since then during our absence from this place we have remitted to you vast sums of money for the due building of such a palace, we do hereby command you to show cause why on our return we find not one stone of that palace placed upon another, not one foundation dug."

ST. THOMAS. [*Quietly.*] Your Majesty mistakes. The palace is being built. Its foundations are secure.

GUNDAPHAR. How so? Show it me, sirrah!

ST. THOMAS. Eye hath not seen it — yet it is here! [*He waves his hand to the circle of the sick and the scholars.*] Hark to what they think of King Gundaphar.

[*Loud cries of* "Long live the King!" "Blessings on the King!" "The Gods protect the King!"]

ST. THOMAS. [*Bending low.*] Sire! you bade me build you a palace, and I have built you one eternal in the heavens.

GUNDAPHAR. [*Stands transfixed for a moment, then says slowly.*] Thou art right, O Saint! It is a palace not made with hands.

[ST. THOMAS *signs to the* CHILDREN; *they go on with their song.*]

There's a palace golden
Storm nor strife can harm,
Where our love is holden
Safe from all alarm.
Day by day we make it,
Not of wood or stone;
None can ever take it,
It is our alone!

— 8 —

THE GOLDEN AGE.

The Golden Age of the Guptas (A.D. 330–455) is the ideal of most Hindus in India. Buddhism had passed away, Brahmanism was in its fullest glory. But it is a curious fact that the greatest king of the whole dynasty

—a marvellous warrior, poet and musician—who conquered all India, is quite unknown to the historians of that country. His lost fame has only come to light of late years by the laborious study of inscriptions and coins. These, however, are extraordinarily copious; so we can form a very good mind-picture of the great Samudragupta, the Napoleon of India.

DRAMATIS PERSONÆ.

SAMUDRAGUPTA, King and Emperor.
HARISHENA, the poet-laureate.
VIKRAMADITYA, the heir-apparent.
THE CEYLON ENVOY.
KALIDASA, a poet.
DHANWANTARI, a physician.
VARAHAMIHIRA, an astronomer.
VARARUCHI, a grammarian.

SCENE.

The Audience-chamber. It is full of high functionaries. The utmost magnificence prevails. To the right and left of the throne stand the 'Nava Ratna' or nine learned men for whom the Court was famous.

SAMUDRAGUPTA. Bid the poet-laureate tell the tale of my glory and renown.

KALIDASA. [*Aside.*] How many false rhymes and halting lines shall we hear from Harishena, I wonder!

VIKRAMADITYA. [*Reprovingly.*] Thou canst not expect a hero like my father—for all that he is no mean poet himself—to be so particular as to prosody as I.

SAMUDRAGUPTA. Yet stay! Before we go on to recount past deeds of glory, there is an envoy from Ceylon to be received. Bid him stand forth.

[*The* CEYLON ENVOY *enters laden with gems, etc.*]

CEYLON ENVOY. Ah, most renowned! Conqueror of Kings! Uprooter of many Rajahs! Foe of the forest tribes! My master, great King Meghavarna of Ceylon, sends these, with a request. The Buddhist pilgrims to Bodh Gaya find it hard to house themselves in comfort. He would ask leave to build a monastery close to the shrine where they could live in peace. It shall be one worthy the realm of great Samudragupta —full three stories high; three towers shall adorn it and the whole be set in gold and various precious stones. This favour do I ask as humble servant, almost as tributary, to the King. [*Presents his gifts.*]

SAMUDRAGUPTA. [*Gratified.*] The request is granted. Harishena! add this name to those the panegyric holds already. [*To* ENVOY.] You will tell your master, Samudragupta and his heir-apparent—where art thou, Vikrama? Stand forth a moment!—send honourable greetings. You will tell him of our Court, of the nine gems—stand forth wise men—

[KALIDASA *and the rest step forward.*]

who glisten in my crown of wisdom. Poets they are, philosophers, grammarians, and such like, physicians and astronomers, for Samudra holds there are more kingdoms to be won than war can conquer. Ask of these nine what question you may choose and they will answer it.

DHANWANTARI. God send, O King! the gentleman does not need the aid of a physician.

VARARUCHI. Or a grammarian to disentangle the meaning of Your Majesty's most clear and gracious message to his master, which we as loyal subjects do approve.

VARAHAMIHIRA. And sure the stars that guide his embassy are all too fortunate and clear to need astronomers to make the dubious plain.

SAMUDRAGUPTA. Well said! well said! What says Kalidasa?

KALIDASA. What shall I say save this? Samudra's sword, friend of his trust, oft tried in times of peril, bright as the heaven's clear azure when the clouds disheartened vanish, and whose keen edge bites remorseless when the whet of battle sets its sharpness, now is laid aside. No worlds are left to conquer and the Sacred Horse has returned unhaltered from its trespassings.

SAMUDRAGUPTA. Bravo, sir Poet! You must have a care, O Harishena! for your laureateship. Let me have more of this horse-sacrifice, I pray thee Kalidasa.

KALIDASA. [*Reciting.*]

Blessed and anointed for his master's fame
Went the grey stallion forth whom none could tame;
For months and years he ranged the country side
Pasturing at will, while, close behind him ride
A band of heroes, ready to defend
His right to come and go. They made swift end
Of any who dared question their king's right;
So, in due time, there dawned that day so bright
When, still unhaltered the brave horse returned,
Its fiery eye with pride and loyalty burned;
And as it paced the flower-strewn temple way,
It tossed its flowing mane as if 'twould say —
Now, O Samudragupta! thou art king
And I myself as sacrifice I bring
To the great gods who gave me this employ,
To make kings or unmake! I die with joy.

[*He bows. Loud plaudits.*

SAMUDRAGUPTA. [*Taking off his ring and giving it to Kalidasa.*] Most excellent! Write the verses down and I will set them fair upon the *vina.* They are worth the sweetest music. So we will defer the panegyric Harishena made until another time. Thy picture, Kalidasa, of the brave horse that gave his life for me excels the tale of all the many kings I have uprooted with my Axe of Death. Yet here I am Samudra, Emperor of all the world.

—9—

THE GIFTINGS OF THE KING.

Good King Harsha, as he is often called, was a very remarkable man, if only because he was the last Hindu King of India who is of any account. After his death, A. D. 647, the annals become confused. The country was broken up into petty states, each quarrelling with the other, until A. D. 1001, when the Muhammadan conquerors appeared. Harsha, who was a son of the Rajah of Thanesvar, fought for five and thirty years before he considered he had been sufficiently victorious. After that he set himself to imitate Asoka, in preaching peace, and succeeded outwardly. Buddhism was decaying; luxury was at its height, religion was almost lost sight of in ritual, and ceremonies overlaid all social life.

The following sketch of the Giftings of the King should show this.

DRAMATIS PERSONÆ.

HARSHA, the King.
RAJYASRI, his widowed sister.
KUMARA, Rajah of Kamarupa.
HIUEN TSANG, a Chinese pilgrim.
THE LORD HIGH TREASURER.
THE CHIEF BRAHMAN.
THE CHIEF PRIEST.
THE BUDDHIST PRIEST.
THE JAIN PRIEST.
BANA, Court panegyrist.
Musicians, Dancers, Attendants.

SCENE.

The sands at the confluence of the Ganges and the Jumna near Allahabad. They are set out as for the Magh Mela which is still celebrated in the same place. The assembly has been going on for days. In one portion an image of Buddha is set up: in another one of Siva, and so on. Buddhist monks and Brahmans jostle one another in friendly fashion. All is good-humoured jollity and popular freedom.

HARSHA. [*Who is holding a canopy over the head of a golden Buddha that is being carried in procession, and who is dressed as the Sun-god, heaving a sigh as his task ends.*] So! that, thank the powers that be, is over. Truly piety of that sort needs thews and sinews for its penances; but it pleases the multitude.

KUMARA. [*Attired as the god Siva, with a fly-whisk with which he diligently fans* HARSHA'S *face.*] True, O King! Your subjects are well off. You give them their choice in deities.

BANA. And they take—none! 'Tis better fun than reading Your Majesty's last play to watch the fashionable families of the Court, making certain of divine support by offering pennyworths of sweets to every supreme Being in turn! Look yonder at General Skandagupta. He wants Your Majesty to give him a command; and see how he prostrates himself before every god in the show! He should have a care of his nose! 'Tis as long as Your Majesty's pedigree.

HARSHA. [*Laughing.*] Wilt leave no one alone, Bana, with thy tongue?

BANA. [*Bowing.*] None, save Your Majesty: and there human tongues are unequal to the task.

HARSHA. Peace! peace! thy quips become wearisome. See, Hiuen Tsang! yonder arrives my sister; so the last act of this drama may begin. Hast found it interesting?

HIUEN TSANG. All things in this wonderful India of yours are worthy of a place in the record I keep of my visits, and these giftings of the King most of all. Yet do I fail so far to see the reason of it.

HARSHA. Simple enough! The whole revenues of this country, a somewhat rich one —

LORD HIGH TREASURER. A very rich one, Mightiness! — come straight to the King's hand. He distributes them; fairly or unfairly depends upon the King.

BANA. This King is both! fair to his subjects, most unfair to himself!

HARSHA. [*Gratified.*] Peace! peace! So, see you. sir Traveller, he is as it were the State pump that gives water to the administration. Now in the process some small or large portion must remain — or — or stick to the pots or hands! Ha! ha! you take me? So to avoid over-richness it has been enacted since ancient days that once every five years an Indian King must strip himself to the skin before his people, as I am going to do to-day. As you have seen I have already given away all else on the previous days; but this is the crowning one. So now to business.

[*Goes out to welcome his sister.*]

HIUEN TSANG. [*To* KUMARA.] Most wonderful! Does the King indeed gift all?

KUMARA. [*With a wink.*] That question had best be asked of the Lord Treasurer. The Crown jewels are curiously alike. [*Enter* RAJYASRI.]

RAJYASRI. Welcome, gentleman! your servant and the servant of the Sun, whom I worship every day, offering to him a bunch of red lotuses set in a pure vessel of ruby, my heart tinged with the same hue. [*Sighs.*]

BANA. Beautiful, most beautiful!

RAJYASRI. Peace be on you, Hiuen Tsang! After this ceremony is over we adjourn to see my brother the King's last operetta, 'The Necklace.' It is full of songs and dances and most entertaining. You will be interested.

HIUEN TSANG. All things, Madam, in this wonderful India of yours— [ATTENDANTS *entering.*]

ATTENDANTS. Peace! peace! Here comes King Harsha to his gifting.

[*Enter* HARSHA *in robes of state. He salutes his sister theatrically, raising her as she falls at his feet.*]

HARSHA. At times like these all human beings are equal. [*Addresses the multitude.*] Ah, my people! I your king renounce all riches. Poor as the poorest must I be before fit worship can be paid to all the Buddhas of all time. [*He tears off his tiara.*] Lo! this, my crown, I give to the Chief Brahman for the use of his most holy temple.

CHIEF BRAHMAN. Great Siva receives it and will surely bless the giver.

HARSHA. And these [*Takes off his necklace and ropes of pearls.*] I give to the great Blessed One whose follower I am.

BUDDHIST PRIEST. And he who lived a life of poverty will take it for religious use.

HARSHA. And these poor trifles [*Removing ear-rings, bracelets, etc.*] do I gift to those who hold the sacredness of life as first of all.

JAIN PRIEST. I do receive them thankfully.

HARSHA. Now there remain but these; *He touches his clothes.*] but how can I, without indecency, appear before you all *sans* clothes?

RAJYASRI. [*Modestly.*] Brother! I have here a mendicant's robe well worn: the man was holy.

BANA. [*Aside.*] So is his garment!

RAJYASRI. If this suffice.

HARSHA. [*Effusively.*] My more than sister! Ever since I lay upon my mother's breast and thou, dear one, didst join thy voice to hers in sweetest lullaby — [*Aside.*] Write that down, Bana, 'twill do for my next verse — ever since then, my counsellor and best protector! Nothing more suitable could, sure, be found. Lo! I am mendicant on all the world for alms.

[*They remove his royal robes and attire him in the mendicant's dress: musicians play, the populace applaud, etc., etc.*]

[*Pompously.*] Now is the sacrifice accomplished and I stand, a man amongst my people.

[*Loud plaudits.*]

So now to worship at the shrine and then, Hiuen Tsang, to supper: that will interest you.

HIUEN TSANG. [*Following.*] All things, Sire, in this wonderful India of yours.

BANA. And this most of all, if thy stomach be as empty as mine!

— 10 —

THE IDOL-BREAKER.

Sultan Mahmud of Ghazni in the year A. D. 1001 began the campaigns of the Crescent which were to last for two centuries. He raided India no less than twelve times. He was a great general and a successful warrior, but the love of gold had gripped at his heart. When he was dying he sent for all the gold and caskets of precious jewels in his treasury and wept because be could not take them with him.

It was of him that the poet Saadi wrote :—

The King of Khurasan saw in a dream
Mahmud the son of Sabaktagin,
Dead for this hundred years or more;
His head, his heart, his arms, his thighs
Dissolved to dust, only his eyes
Moved in their sockets and saw
His gold, his empire, everything
He loved, in the hands of another King.

A terrible punishment, truly even for such a man!

DRAMATIS PERSONÆ.

SULTAN MAHMUD, of Ghazni.
HIS GENERAL.
A CAPTAIN OF THE GUARD.
MASUD KHAN, the Sultan's son.
MAHOMED KHAN, the Sultan's son.
A MOHUNT.
THE CHIEF BRAHMAN.
A BRAHMAN.
AN ACOLYTE.
Soldiers, etc., etc.

SCENE.

The Temple at Somnath. It stands on the edge of the sea, the tides of which as they rise and fall are supposed to be adoring the great lingam in the Sanctuary within. This is arched and has fifty-six pillars curiously carved and gilt and richly ornamented with precious stones. It has no light, except that which streams from the doorway and the feeble flicker of a lamp hung by a golden chain that weighs fifteen hundred pounds and which also supports a huge golden bell. The lingam is really a black upright stone pillar such as is seen in many temples now-a-days, but it is cased in gold and rises ten feet above the floor. The temple is empty, but there is noise of confused fighting without.

ACOLYTE. [*Running across.*] We are lost, we are lost, the enemy is at hand!

CHIEF BRAHMAN [*Entering calmly.*] Peace, boy! [*He takes hold of the golden chain and clangs the bell. It echoes out, drowning the noise of battle.*] Great Siva!

Giver of Life and Death, hear, oh, hear. Protect Thy temple and protect Thyself [*He passes to the door and looks out. Exultantly.*] See ! He hears, the battle slackens. Ah ! thanks to Thee, great Siva. Yonder are the pennants of Anhalwara. The reinforcements have arrived. The impious Mussulmans waver. Ah, great Siva ! to Thy shrine I vow a thousand golden ingots. [*He stands watching.*]

[*Suddenly a loud raucous voice is heard.*]

VOICE. Allah-hu-akbar ! Allah-i-hu ! Smite down Thy foes. Destroy the idolaters. Lo ! prostrate before Thee, I call for victory. Din ! Din ! Futteh Mahomed ! Futteh Mahomed !

[*The noise of fighting grows louder.*]

MOHUNT. [*Entering hastily.*] All is lost, the outcast dogs win. Let us save what we can. [*He advances to the golden lingam, then holds back, for the foe darts through the door. They stand amazed.*]

CAPTAIN OF THE GUARD. By God and His Prophet, saw I never the like. Look at yon chain ! Solid gold, I'll warrant me. [*He spits.*] Curses on the idolaters.

[*His men prod the chain with their pikes.*]

SOLDIERS. Ay ! solid gold. [*They spit.*] Curses on the idolaters. And this—[*They prod the lingam.*] think you, it is solid gold !

CAPTAIN OF THE GUARD. Hands off ! The Sultan comes. Hands off, I say !

[*Enter* MAHMUD *and staff. The temple fills up ; on one side Mussulmans, on the other Brahmans.*]

MAHMUD. [*Solemnly spitting.*] Stand aside, idolatrous dogs ! and let me see the idol. So that is your god, is it? By the Prophet, what fools men be! And all this wealth [*He looks round.*] wasted,—on what? Bah! There is no world that we can touch save this, and here gold is all!

BRAHMAN. [*Hastily.*] It is not real gold, 'tis but stone gilt over.

MAHMUD. [*Scowling.*] Gold or gilt, it shall be destroyed. Bid the mace-men hither. They shall smite at it, and one piece shall go to Holy Mecca and one will I tread upon as threshold to my palace at Ghazni. So much for thy god.

[*He spurns with his feet the pile of jasmine and marigold chaplets that lie at the foot of the lingam.*]

CHIEF BRAHMAN. [*Prostrating himself.*] Hold! I beseech thee, mighty conqueror. Lo! thou hast overcome us. I and my god lie in the dust before thee. What is gained by further sacrifice? Surely naught. But if thy hand will spare this stone at which thou mockest, we, its priests, will pay two maunds of solid gold.

MAHMUD. Of solid gold? Stupendous! but I will not.

BRAHMAN. Say not so. Bethink thee, conqueror. This stone to us is even so as thy God is to thee, as holy, sacred. Leave it, O great King! to us and to our worship.

CAPTAIN OF THE GUARD. [*With subdued deference.*] The man speaks well. God is above us all, the one, the same: we see Him different. That is all.

BRAHMAN. Oh, thanks, my friend. Thou voicest my thought. Our God, as yours, bids you have mercy.

MAHMUD. No! no! idolatrous fool. Here, mace-bearers.

CHIEF BRAHMAN. [*Aside.*] Peace, Govind; he cares not for that God: his god is gold! [*Aloud.*] Sir! if thou grant this mercy all the gold, nay fifteen maunds, shall be delivered here.

MAHOMED KHAN. Father! bethink thee. Fifteen maunds means much; 'tis more than a king's ransom, and thrice over more than that poor stone.

MASUD KHAN. My brother speaks the truth. Had I the choice, I'd choose the gold and leave the fools to their own folly.

MAHOMED KHAN. Yea! so would I; for see you, virtue might be gained by breaking the vile idol, but far more by giving of the gold to those who need it. To my mind, 'tis one poor idol out of millions in this land, against the succour of the Faithful poor.

MAHMUD. [*Frowning.*] What you say is true; the gold is great — [*Hesitates.*] and yet, were I to make this bargain with the priests, my name would stand "Mahmud the idol-seller"! Better far — [*He raises his hand which holds a mace.*]

MOHUNT. [*Wildly.*] Beware! O man of blood, beware! He who gives life can take it.

MAHMUD. [*Fiercely.*] What! thou defiest me? Then away with thoughts of traffic. I shall be called "Mahmud the idol-breaker"! [*He smites the lingam once, twice, thrice.*]

[*The outer shell of gold breaks and a hoard of perfectly priceless jewels rolls out and heaps itself at his feet.*]

[*Cries of* 'Bismillah' *from the Mussulmans.*]

[*The Hindus stand stupefied.*]

[*Sanctimoniously.*] The most Merciful hath protected His own. These must be worth at least one hundred maunds of gold. Praise to the All-powerful!

—11—

THE RESISTANCE OF THE RAJPUTS.

More than a hundred years after the Idol-breaker had clutched at India, Mahomed Ghori followed his example and came down like a whirlwind from the western mountains. But the first time he came he found the Rajput princes united and prepared, and met with a smashing defeat. He returned, however, to the charge after two years and was successful, defeating Prithvi-Raj and the flower of Rajput chivalry. The story of Prithvi-Raj and the fair Princess Samyukta is a wonderful romance, and the words with which she sent her husband out to his last fight with the Mahomedan conqueror should be learnt by heart by every Indian boy and girl. They would make them understand the part they are severally to play in the great drama of Life. For this purpose they have been introduced into this playlet.

DRAMATIS PERSONÆ.

PRITHVI-RAJ.
CHAWAND RAO, Prithvi's brother.
THE RAJAH OF KANAUJ, Prithvi's brother-in-law.
THE RAJAH OF ULWAR, Prithvi's cousin.
THE RAJAH OF BIANA, Prithvi's ally.
CHAND, a Bard.
Rajput Nobles, a Messenger, Soldiers.

SCENE.

A tent outside the pink and white fortress at Bhatinda. [*It is evening.*]

[PRITHVI-RAJ *seated*, CHAWAND RAO *standing.*]

CHAWAND RAO. Thou art dull, brother. Wherefore so? Is not our army nigh ten times stronger than it was when we drove the infamous outcaste from Hindostan last time? Have we not a backing of a hundred and fifty brave Rajput Rajahs, and over 300,000 horsemen, to say nothing of 3,000 elephants, and a large body of infantry? Where is the cause for fear?

PRITHVI. [*Smiling.*] Fear? 'Tis well it is my brother, Chawand, who uses that word to one who knows it not. Nay, brother! Prithvi is no coward. But see you; what time you, a mere lad, lost your front teeth in that encounter with Shahab-ud-din himself, we Rajputs were as one. They followed my lead and asked no other. Now it is otherwise. Each day an army council sits, and I scarce seem to know what goes on at the four corners of this vast camp.

MESSENGER. The Rajah of Kanauj craves audience.

PRITHVI. With all honour.

[*Enter* KANAUJ.]

Welcome! brother-in-law. What news?

KANAUJ. Only the old tale about Biana's kettle-drums that must go first. These old traditions and old accoutrements hamper us much.

PRITHVI. They do. Yet with them come the old honour, the old devotions, the old chivalry, the old truth. The Rajputs could not wish it otherwise.

MESSENGER. The Rajah of Ulwar craves audience.

PRITHVI. With all honour.

[*Enter* ULWAR.]

All hail! cousin. How goes it?

ULWAR. Well, only Biana's kettledrums stand in the way.

CHAWAND RAO. [*Laughing.*] Let them stand. Were I my brother I should get rid of them.

MESSENGER. The Rajah of Biana craves audience.

PRITHVI. With all honour.

CHAWAND RAO. Now, brother, you will have to settle the kettles!

PRITHVI. Peace! 'tis no laughing matter.

[*Enter* BIANA.]

BIANA. I have come to ask why —

PRITHVI. By your leave, friend, there is matter more important. Two hours ago we held an army council. You were not there, so you may like to know that, by covenant, seeing that our forces so far outnumber the enemy, I despatched a letter to their leader calling on him to surrender. It seemed the only honourable course. The letter ran thus:

"To the bravery of the Rajputs you are no stranger. To our vast superiority in numbers, your eyes bear witness. If you yourself are weary of life, have pity on your troops who may still desire to live. Repent therefore of the rash enterprise you have undertaken and we shall permit you to retreat in safety."

ULWAR, BIANA AND ALL. Well done! We could do no less. Well done!

ULWAR. And the answer?

PRITHVI. I expect it every moment.

MESSENGER. The envoy hath returned from the camp of the enemy.

PRITHVI. Bid him enter.

[*Enter* ENVOY *with nobles and soldiers. He presents a letter.* PRITHVI *takes it.*]

CHAWAND RAO. What does he say, brother?

PRITHVI. [*Reading.*] "From Mahomed Shahab-ud-din, Generalissimo of the Mussulman forces. Being but the General in command I dare not retreat without orders, therefore I crave a truce till such time as I can receive instructions from my brother, the King in Ghazni."

BIANA. A fortnight's truce at least; it will take more than that to get reply.

ULWAR. We shall lose in number by it. The men are keen on fighting. If disappointed they will go.

PRITHVI. And little loss. Such fellows are bad fighters. We had better accept. What say you gentlemen?

RAJPUT NOBLES AND ALL. Ay! a fortnight's truce.

PRITHVI. [*Standing up.*] So be it. Send word that we accept the terms, Chawand.

CHAWAND RAO. It shall be done forthwith; and then for the best night's rest I've had for days. No fear of night alarms.

ULWAR. [*Going.*] My men will be glad of one at any rate. How they will stand fourteen is another matter.

[*They all go.*]

PRITHVI. [*Calls.*] Chand. [*The* BARD *appears.*]

Chand, I am weary, and yet sleep seems far from me. Sing me of old kings, old times. It may soothe me. [*He flings himself on a couch.*]

[CHAND *takes a vina and strikes a few chords, then begins to chant.*]

Hark-hist!
To the list
Of the Kings who have died
In their pride:
To the wide, wide world.
Chand Singh he dreamt he was King
But he died in his pride;
Jai Singh he dreamt he was King
Till he died in his pride:
To the wide, wide world.

[*The music becomes louder.*]

But the dreaming of Kings has no end,
It lives and it never dies:
The spirit of Kings lives for ever,
'Tis the spirit of slaves that dies!

[PRITHVI *sleeps,* CHAND *bends over him.*]

CHAND. Sleep on, master; thy memory will never die.

[*He steals away.*]

PRITHVI. [*In his sleep.*] Wife, dearest one, my counsellor, my friend! what didst thou say? Say it again. Shall I go forth to fight? Yea! yea! bind on my sword, dearest. What didst thou say?

A VOICE. [*From behind.*]

What fool asks woman for advice? The world
Holds her wit shallow. Even when the truth
Comes from her lips, men stop their ears and smile.
And yet, without the woman where is man?
We hold the power of Form; for us the fire
Of Siv's creative force flames up and burns.

Lo! we are thieves of Life, and sanctuaries
Of Souls. Beloved! we share your lives,
Your failures, your successes, griefs and joys.
Hunger and thirst, if yours, are ours, and Death
Parts us not from you; for we follow fast
To serve you in the mansions of the blest.
Sun of the Chauhans? Who hath drunk so deep
Of glory and of pleasure as my lord?
And yet the destiny of all is death:
Yea! even of the gods: and to die well
Is life immortal. Therefore draw your sword,
Smite down the foes of Hind; think not of self:
The garment of this life is frayed and worn.
Think not of me; we twain shall be as one
Hereafter and for ever. Go, my King!

PRITHVI. [*Sleeping.*] Yea, I go; [*A pause; mutters.*] and yet the destiny of all is death! [*A pause.*] I go, wife! I go.

[*A long silence.*]

[*Suddenly a bugle call, drums beat; confused noise.*]

[PRITHVI *starts up, his hand on his sword.*]

CHAWAND RAO. [*Rushing in.*] They are attacking all along the front. Quick!

PRITHVI. But the truce?

CHAWAND RAO. What care the circumcised dogs for honour? Not that it matters. [*Laughs gaily.*] I go to avenge my teeth!

[*Rushes out.*]

PRITHVI. [*Stands.*] The cowards! the liars! [*Draws his sword.*] Samyukta! wife! I go to avenge Truth.

[*Rushes out.*]

[*Confused drums, bugles, sounds of fighting.*]

— 12 —

THE BUILDERS.

The Mahomedan conqueror, Mahomed Ghori, left his favourite slave as King-Governor of Delhi. His real name was Aibak but he called himself Kutb-ud-din, and it was he who ordered the building of that marvellous monument, the Kutb Minar, which stands fourteen miles from Delhi. It is counted as one of the wonders of the world, but the chief wonder about it is too seldom realised; namely that it should have been built, as it was, by Hindu architects out of the ruins and fragments of Hindu temples. The following playlet shows what must have been in their minds while so occupied.

DRAMATIS PERSONÆ.

KUTB, king and slave.	2ND STONEMASON.
GHIASS, his minister.	3RD STONEMASON.
THE HINDU ARCHITECT.	AN OLD ENLAYER.
1ST STONEMASON.	AN APPRENTICE.

Workmen.

SCENE.

A narrow yard. At one side, slowly rising in all its massive beauty, the plinth of the Kutb. Cranes for lifting stones; stonemasons at work, etc.

1ST STONEMASON. [*Singing as he chips away.*]

Good stone and good steel
Aid me in my task;
Fair and square, for woe or weal,
Shaping as I ask,
House and temple both will bring
Flash of fire as hammers ring;
Fire from the great Unknown,
Good steel and good stone.

2ND STONEMASON. 'Tis a good old song doubtless; but 'tis not house or temple now-a-days, 'tis mosque or temple. Curse them!

3RD STONEMASON. Yet do they pay us fair to work fair, so work we must.

2ND STONEMASON. God knows! Sometimes when I shape one of the temple stones to fit yon minaret of a mosque—so they call it—I feel inclined to hammer up and have at it once and for all. 'Tis sacrilege.

OLD ENLAYER. [*Gently.*] I know not, friend. See, here I sit with my black and white marble, as I sate with the red sandstone of old; but 'tis the same work. 'Tis in praise of someone better than I, and the architect knows his work. See here he comes and with him he whom they call King now-a-days. Hai! hai! there be many kings on this earth.

1ST STONEMASON. Peace! Cease chattering or there will be trouble.

[*Enter* KUTB-UD-DIN, GHIASS *and* SRI ANAND *the architect.*]

KUTB. Then thou art sure it will be beautiful, that the proportions are correct.

ARCHITECT. I am sure. I can see it rising, a lance shaft into the clear blue of Heaven. So I dreamed it, so it will be for ever, and ever and ever — beautiful exceedingly.

KUTB. [*Gratified.*] And I shall be remembered, I who built it!

ARCHITECT. [*Smiling.*] Memory is not short for Kings, Your Majesty.

GHIASS. [*Angrily.*] What meanest thou, slave?

ARCHITECT. I am no slave of thine, Sir Minister! Thy master set me this task and I have done it well. The world will forget me, but they will wonder who dreamt the dream of beauty.

KUTB. Leave him alone, Ghiass! He means well, and it looks well what he has done. Truly yon lettering is fine.

ARCHITECT. It will be finer when 'tis finished. It needs now but one stone in its place and the storey is finished.

KUTB. Ha! Could it not be placed now?

ARCHITECT. I will see. [*Crosses to the* old ENLAYER.] Hast finished thy task, O artificer?

OLD ENLAYER. [*Beaming.*] Master! 'tis done, line for line, curve for curve, to the design. Yea! though I know naught of what I do, it is true to what I see. Is it not, O master of arts?

ARCHITECT. It could not be better.

OLD ENLAYER. Giver of Life! all praise for gifting me with deft hands. Now am I satisfied.

ARCHITECT. Here, you there! Overseer, set men to work and heave this stone to its place.

[*The* WORKMEN *heave and lift, set the crane, etc. As they do it they sing.*]

Each to its place,
Hil-lil-lo!
So it shall face,
Hil-lil-lo!
Close to its neighbour.
Hurry there! our labour,
Must not be slow.
O Hil-lil-lo!
Other stones are ready
Waiting us. O steady,
Not so fast below.
Hil-lil-lo!

[*The stone falls to its place amid plaudits.*]

KUTB. Ay! that perfects it. If all goes as well as that, Sir Architect, men will not forget me.

[*Goes*]

ARCHITECT. [*Softly.*] And the world will not forget beauty.

[GHIASS *is going when the* old ENLAYER *stops him.*]

OLD ENLAYER. Sir, I am old and I am not learned in your tongue. Yet have I written it yonder in fair lettering and good stone. I pray you tell me what it means.

GHIASS. [*Carelessly.*] There is but one God and—

KUTB. [*Without.*] Ghiass, I say Ghiass.

GHIASS. I come, my lord.

[*Exit hurriedly.*]

OLD ENLAYER. [*Exultantly setting to work on a fresh slab.*] Said I not so, brothers? There is but one God, and we praise him when we work fair and truly.

[*Sits and sings in an old cracked voice as he works.*]

One are they all!
Ears that hear aright,
Eyes that see the light,
Hands of power and might;
One are they all,
Light, and might and right!

—13—

THE STRATEGY OF PADMANI.

The great sack of Chitor in 1303 is one of the most striking episodes of Indian History. It shows us the martial Rajput race, driven to bay by superior forces, sacrificing itself, the flower of its chivalry, its very women, sooner than accepting defeat. And one of the finest incidents in the long struggle which ended in the supreme sacrifice of the *Johar*, is the trick played by Queen Padmani by which she rescued her husband from the clutches of Ala-ud-din the Mahomedan Commander-in-Chief, afterwards King.

DRAMATIS PERSONÆ.

RAJAH BHIMSI, Padmani's husband, Regent of Chitor.

ALA-UD-DIN, the Mahomedan Commander-in-Chief.

A MAHOMEDAN OFFICER.

Rajput Nobles and Soldiers.

SCENE.

A tent outside the fortress of Chitor. A guard stands at the door. It is night.

[BHIMSI *and* ALA-UD-DIN.]

BHIMSI. Yea! I am in your power. That I admit. But why? Have I not faithfully fulfilled the contract made between us?—Ay, to the letter! Am I not a Rajput? Is not honour dearer to me than life? I bartered safety to my ward the young King, safety to his people, for what to me was outrage horrible. You, having heard of my wife's peerless beauty, asked for a sight of her, and I refused. I had no choice. Death was preferable to dishonour.

ALA-UD-DIN. [*Nonchalantly.*] Surely I have heard this before.

BHIMSI. [*Vehemently.*] And you shall hear it again! Then you asked to see but the reflection of her dear face in a mirror. I bid her decide, and she said, "Yea! God's light will come between me and lustful eyes; that is sufficient screen for virtue." So it was done. You looked your fill. And then, dead to all honour, you bade your minions overpower me and carry me off a hostage.

ALA-UD-DIN. [*With a laugh.*] A very efficient one too! Your wife, fair Lady Padmani—her beauty was not exaggerated; she is peerless—has consented to rescue you, the Regent of Chitor, the man without whom defence is impossible, by placing herself in my hands. The exchange is good for me, and good for Chitor and you. Well! the lady has made her fair choice and there is no more to be said.

BHIMSI. Were my hands not tied I would have at you, most infamous! save that I would scarce soil my Rajput hands with the blood of such carrion.

ALA-UD-DIN. Easy! sir, easy! Or I may not keep my word in letting you go when the lady comes; and I would fain do that, since she comes to me of her own free will.

BHIMSI. I refuse to believe it.

ALA-UD-DIN. [*Shrugging his shoulders.*] I await her even now. She and her maidens—fifty litters full—all with due privacy. Ah! I will treat her well, you need not fear.

BHIMSI. [*Groaning.*] Ah! for my sword.

ALA-UD-DIN. You will have it ere long. The litters take you back.

[*Enter* OFFICER.]

OFFICER. Sire, the torch-bearers show on the outskirts of the camp.

ALA-UD-DIN. Good. See that the passage is clear of all men, and the troops have been sent to quarters.

OFFICER. Ay, sir, all is private.

[*Exit.*]

ALA-UD-DIN. Come, my friend, it will soon be over. Hark to the jingle of the litters. They are in the court. [*Starts up.*] Hist! what is that?

[*Confused shouting, then silence.*]

OFFICER. [*Running in.*] My lord! my lord! The litters have belched forth armed men They have overpowered the guards and gagged them. They are here. Save yourself while there is yet time.

ALA-UD-DIN. I—I—

[SOLDIERS *appear at the door, there is a short struggle with the* GUARDS, *then silence.*]

[*Trying to escape at back of tent.*] Curses on the woman. She has outwitted me.

BHIMSI. Padmani! my peerless wife.

THE RAJPUTS. [*Surround him.*] Quick, my lord! to the litters, to the litters. All is arranged. We will fight our way back if need be. Quick! quick!

[*Exeunt, leaving the* GUARDS *gagged.*]

—14—

THE INVASION OF TIMUR.

It was about the year A. D. 1200 that Aibak the Slave founded the first Mahomedan dynasty in Delhi. For close on two hundred years one dynasty followed the other. Dissension became rife, governor quarrelled with governor, provinces were split up, and the time was ripe for rebellion or invasion. The latter came. Timur, "the lame firebrand of the world," a descendant of Chingiz Khan the Tartar, who, a hundred and fifty years before, had swept like a scorching flame over north-west Asia, saw his opportunity and took it. He writes in his Memoirs: "Learnt that the people of India were at variance one with the other. Their conquest appeared to me easy. Resolved to undertake it and make myself master of the Indian Empire. Did so."

This laconic summary is absolutely true. He devastated India, took from it untold plunder and returned leaving it desolate.

DRAMATIS PERSONÆ.

TIMUR.
CAPTAIN OF A TROOP.
1ST VILLAGER.
2ND VILLAGER.
3RD VILLAGER.
AN OLD GRANDMOTHER.
JAIMUL, a herd boy.

Troopers, etc.

SCENE.

A village hut a few miles outside Delhi. It is empty save for an old grandmother stirring the embers of a fire with a stick. A pile of chupatties is keeping warm by the fire, the pot of dhal simmers gently, a ghurra of fresh water stands on the floor. It is evidently nigh dinner time.

GRANDMOTHER. [*Mumbling and chanting.*]

When I was a lassie I mind me,
Mother would say, were I over-bold,
" The Toork, the Toork he will find you
If ye don't do as you're told ;
If you don't do as you're told,
The Toork, the Toork he will find you ! "

Ay ! ay ! that was a long time ago, but it serves to frighten the bairns still. Mercy on us ! What is that ?

[*Running footsteps outside, two men burst in.*]

1ST VILLAGER. The Toork ! the Toork ! Quick, buddhi, quick ! Gather the women together. Away with them into the jungle. Quick, I say ! There is no time to be lost. The Toork is upon us.

[*He begins to rummage for valuables in the walls.*]

GRANDMOTHER. [*Feebly.*] The Toork ! But he must be dead long ago. It was in my grandmother's time he came.

2ND VILLAGER. Peace, grandam! There is no time for thine ancient twaddle. Go, get the women together. I tell thee I saw them with my own eyes like a horde of locusts, devouring all things. Go, I say, go! [*She hurries off mouthing.*] Hast all the silver? Quick or we are lost!

3RD VILLAGER. [*Bursting in.*] There is no sign of Jaimul.

1ST VILLAGER. Jaimul must fend for himself. A man can but save his own skin. Quick! they come, they come.

[*All rush out; a slight pause, then a band of* TROOPERS *rush in, dashing here and there in search of something.*]

CAPTAIN. What! No women? They have been too quick for us here. But at any rate there is dinner and drink.

[*The* TROOPERS *snatch off the pot, seize the chupatties and eat heartily.*]

Come! I feel better. I was half done with hunger and thirst.

[*The door opens and in walks a lame man, clad as they are, in trooper's dress. There is great consternation and they all fall to attention.*]

TIMUR. [*With a sharp glance round.*] What! guzzling when your orders were to pillage as far as Amarkot. This will be remembered against you. Sir Captain, I forget your name.

CAPTAIN. Fateh-din, Sire.

TIMUR. There will be little victory for the Faith with such as you. Consider yourself degraded. March and obey your orders. [*Exeunt all.*]

[TIMUR *looks in the pot and in the ghurra.*]

And not one crumb or drop left! Curses on them. But I would have done the same myself had I been they, and thought nothing of my master being starved. [*He seats himself and stirs the embers as the old grandmother had stirred them.*] Well! my task is nigh done. The Toork has come with a vengeance to Hindustan once more. These miserable pagans will not forget it for a hundred years, not they!

[*The door opens and in comes* JAIMUL, *a lad about ten, bearing in his hand a lotah full of milk.*]

JAIMUL. Here is the milk, grandam. [*Starts and makes to run away.*]

TIMUR. Didst say milk, jackanapes? Bring it here.

JAIMUL. [*Hesitating.*] It is not mine to give.

TIMUR. [*With a hard laugh.*] Ha! is it not? Then I'll take it.

[*Unsheaths his sword, then on second thoughts lays it on a shelf; strides over to the boy, seizes the milk, gives* JAIMUL *a cuff that sends him reeling, then drains the lotah in great gulps.*]

[JAIMUL *stands, his hand to his ear, but defiant.*]

Bless thy stars, boy, that my thirst was too great to admit of time to kill thee; and now, having drunk of thy milk, I dare not. Besides thou art a brave cockerel. Had I my men with me thou shouldst come with me and be a circumcised Mahomedan instead of a hell-doomed pagan. Yet forget not that thou hast seen Timur the Toork and that he spared thy life. 'Tis not many can tell that tale.

[*Sheaths his sword and strides out.*]

[*The old* GRANDMOTHER *returns and crouches by the fire, once more stirring the embers.*]

GRANDMOTHER. [*To herself.*] They went too fast. They were young and I am old. But the Toork will not find me, I am too old. No, no. [*Begins to sing.*]

When I was a lassie I mind me,
Mother would say, were I over-bold,
"The Toork, the Toork he will find you—"

JAIMUL. [*Interrupting.*] Grandam! I have seen him.

GRANDMOTHER. Seen whom?

JAIMUL. Timur the Toork.

—15—

THE PLEDGE.

The founder of the Mughal dynasty was Babur, whose real name was Zahir-ud-din Mahomed. His grandfather gave him the nickname which means 'Tigercub,' because, being a rough and ready old Toork, he objected to his grandson's high sounding names. Babur is one of the most lovable characters to be found in any history. He ascended the throne at eleven years of age, and until his death led the most adventurous life it is possible to imagine. He was the first Western to make India his home. Other conquerors, frightened at the extreme heat, left it more or less to the hands of viceroys and agents: Babur governed it himself. He was a tall handsome man, no mean poet, an excellent musician, and his Autobiography is one of the most interesting books ever written. It tells the truth, no more, no less.

The following incident took place just before Babur's last great battle with the Rajput General Rana Sanga, which left him master of Hindustan.

DRAMATIS PERSONÆ

BABUR, the King.
HUMAYUN, the King's son.
TARDI BEG, a soldier dervish.
ASAS, the heaviest drinker in camp.
MAHDI KHWAJA, Babur's son-in-law.
MAHOMED SHARIF, an astrologer.
Sentries, soldiers.

SCENE.

A camp near Fatehpur Sikri. In front the King's tent. It is closed. Two sentries guard it. It is dawn.

1st SENTRY. [*Yawning.*] Ha! it grows chill in the dawn. 'Twill be good when the watch is over.

2nd SENTRY. 'Twill not be long now. There goes a *nakarah.* The parade is for five of the day.

1st SENTRY. Ay! What for? I wonder. To roast us for listening to the astrologer, mayhap!

2nd SENTRY. For our good anyhow. Never was such a man as Babur for heartening up courage. Mind you when we were all for going back Kabulwards and he up and spoke to us? I see him now, his eyes all ablaze. "Let none who calls himself my friend ever talk of turning tail; but if any lack the courage to stay, let him go! I want him not." And see you, not one of us stirred; we were all his friends.

[*The tent opens.* BABUR *and* TARDI BEG *come out.*]

BABUR. [*Saluting.*] You have leave. Babur defends himself when he is awake.

TARDI BEG. God send it may be so ever! yet this astrologer says—

BABUR. [*Kindly but quickly.*] Nay! nay! not from *you,* best of friends. Leave that to the ignorant. Truly God's stars war against no man who does his duty. [*He pauses.*] And therein lies the gist of the matter. See you, Tardi Beg—friend of how many years as *dervish* or soldier—when the astrologer began frightening my soldiers with tales of the opposition of Mars I was full angered and called him a villainous soothsayer, as he is. Then thought came; and thought brought wisdom. I asked of myself, Am I doing my duty? and lo! the answer was, Thou art not. Art thou not often half drunk, nay! whole drunk—what gain is there in untruth—with wine? Dost thou not eat drugged comfits? Are these the actions of a pious Mussulman? And granted thou hast excuse—and God knows I have some—didst thou not promise thyself to give up the habit when thou wast forty years of age? And art thou not five and forty, O Zahir-ud-din Mahomed Babur? And so, in a second, friend—like a flash of God's lightning—I saw. I saw that I had been cheating myself, that I had been cheating my God. So now there must be truth between us, uttermost truth. This day that comes so fast [*stretches his hand out*]—see, how yon drift of spent rose-leaf clouds lies between the lightening earth and the lightening sky; see how their curled petals catch the underglow of the unrisen sun; is it not wonderful?—this day may bring defeat or it may bring victory. But it shall bring truth and courage. [*Enter* HUMAYUN. *They salute as dear friends.*]

HUMAYUN. The troops are massing for the parade, father. What news i' the night? Is there chance of attack?

BABUR. The outposts are quiet. Rana Sanga is cautious. We have to do with a wily old fox, my son. Lo! Humayun, the very sight of thee makes my heart open like a rosebud. [*Enter* MAHDI KHWAJA. *He salutes.*]

MAHDI KHWAJA. Good morrow, most beloved! There is word from thy daughter, my wife. She prays for victory and prosperity.

BABUR. Little Ma'asuma! Well, she shall have it if these hands can compass it. And now to make ready.

[*Retires to tent. Enter* ASAS.]

ASAS. God be thanked I am in time for this parade; but half a skin of good Shiraz at midnight makes one drowsy at the dawn. And wherefore is it called? I fain would know that.

[*Enter* MAHOMED SHARIF *between two sentries.*]

MAHOMED SHARIF. Wherefore? Because I read the stars; because I gave the warning. Babur will punish me before his army. But the truth, the truth will show with time.

TARDI BEG. Peace, fool! If 'tis the truth, 'twill come without thy telling.

HUMAYUN. There come the troops, Asas. Bid them form a half circle there on the plain before us.

[*Exit* ASAS.]

MAHDI KHWAJA. Rana Sanga can have no finer troops than these.

HUMAYUN. True, but he hath three to our one.

TARDI BEG. [*Softly.*] Were we all as thy father, O my prince! that would be more than even. Are they all assembled? Then I will call the King.

[*A pause, bugles, drums, nakaras.*]

[*The tent opens and* BABUR *appears in a plain white robe, in his right hand a crystal drinking cup.*]

BABUR. Noblemen, Gentlemen, Soldiers. All who sit down to the feast of Life must end by drinking the cup of Death. Therefore it behoves each of us to be ready for the last draught by repenting him of the evil he has done. Lo! I repent me of my sin. I repent me of my broken promise. Now, with the salvation of a righteous death close to me, I cast away my great temptation. [*He flings away the crystal cup.*] Lo! I repent. Who follows me?

[*A minute's pause.*]

ASAS. I do, Sire.

BABUR. That makes it the less hard, Asas, old boon companion. Thou hast more to renounce than I.

TARDI BEG. I also, O most clement, I follow fair wherever Babur goes.

BABUR. Thanks! best of friends.

MAHDI KHWAJA. And I.

HUMAYUN. And I.

[*A confused shouting,* 'And I,' 'And I,' 'And I,' *from the thousands of unseen soldiers. The officers press forward holding their swords in homage. General enthusiasm.*]

BABUR. [*Joyfully.*] Lo! we are as one now. And as one man will we fight the foe. God's stars do not war against a righteous cause. Lo! the Most High will be merciful to us. So let us swear that none of us will turn his face from Death or Victory till his soul be separated from his body. As the poet says—

With fame, though I die, I am content;
Let fame be mine, though life be spent.

[*A roar of assent fill the air.*]

[*The sun rises.*]

—16—

A CHILD'S MEMORY.

Humayun, Babur's son, was through his own faults — he was an inveterate opium-eater — ousted from his kingdom for years. His son, afterwards to be the great Akbar, was born in exile. The following incident, which is strictly historical, shows both these facts distinctly.

DRAMATIS PERSONÆ.

HUMAYUN, the Emperor.
AKBAR, his little son aged four.
MIRZA HINDAL, Humayun's brother.
MIRZA YADGAR NASIR, Humayun's brother.
BAIRAM KHAN, General and Minister.
NADIM KHAN, Akbar's foster-father.
CHAMBERLAIN.

SCENE IN KABUL.

The dais set for a garden festivity as viewed from the audience. Draperies, coloured lamps, carpets, etc.

[NADIM KHAN *and* CHAMBERLAIN.]

NADIM KHAN. If the child knows not his mother 'twill be small wonder. He was but fifteen months old that dreary night in the desert when my lady Queen Hamida, her face bathed in tears, left him to our charge. Ay! ay! a weary dreary day, and a weary dreary three years since then.

CHAMBERLAIN. But now all goes well. My lord King Humayun is victorious over all his enemies, and the years of disgrace and wandering seem to have passed him by. He is merry and handsome as ever, and as full of quips and cranks. Who but he would have thought of setting a little lad of four to the recognizing of his mother, and having thought of it, have devised such a festivity as this? Lo! it will be like the day of resurrection. Yonder wide balcony that will be filled with ladies of distinction all veiled in green — the birds in cages among the trees, that will set up a piping if the little prince's memory be good enough to choose his mother aright — and the Emperor himself, and the musicians! Lo! my brain grows crazy with the thought of all that has to be arranged. [*Fusses off.*]

[*Enter* MIRZA HINDAL *and* BAIRAM KHAN.]

HINDAL. Good morrow, foster-father. We would be alone.

NADIM KHAN. At your pleasure, sirs. [*Goes.*] What schemes are they up to now, I wonder? Truly, after one has been on edge for nigh four years, guarding an infant life from wicked men, one learns to suspect all things on God's earth. [*Exit listening.*]

HINDAL. So far, so good. My brother's star is in the ascendant, for the time. And it behoves wise men to accept the decree of Providence. But if once more Humayun's fortunes should follow his wild wits, what then?

BAIRAM KHAN. With all due deference, Mirza Sahib, I leave that for time to answer. Here comes the Emperor and his son. By the Prophet, a most likely lad! Look at his grave eyes, his firm mouth.

My lady Khanzada Khanum was right when she said he favoured his grandfather more than his father. I mind me, when a lad myself, seeing just that same steady gaze when Babur came to audience. Most clement and merciful! your servant.

[*They bow to* HUMAYUN *and little* AKBAR *who are followed by standard-bearers, guards, nobles and* NADIM KHAN. HUMAYUN *seats himself on throne. Little* AKBAR *shows an inclination to take his foster-father's hand.*]

HUMAYUN. [*Laughing.*] Nay! nay! stand of thyself, sonling. So, right in the middle all alone, quite alone. Thou'lt find Amma-jan before long, I'll warrant. So here we are, gentlemen, as comfortable as if the past years of fighting were a dream. I and my brothers—[*He looks affectionately towards* HINDAL *and* YADGAR NASIR.] reconciled: [*His face clouds.*] only Kamran and Askari absent. But they will come in and my beloved father's wish be realised that we brothers should not quarrel. So now to business. Akbar, my son! Thou seest that row of ladies of the highest distinction discreetly veiled in green. From amongst them thou must choose thy mother.

AKBAR. [*In a loud resonant grave voice.*] But I do not see any faces, father, the veils are all alike!

HUMAYUN. [*Laughing.*] So wilt thou see thy bride in the future, sonling. But these ladies will raise their veils when I give the order. Art ready, son?

AKBAR. [*His lips trembling.*] Father, I would rather not.

NADIM KHAN. 'Fore heaven it is a shame! How can a child remember all these years?

BAIRAM KHAN. Peace, fool! I'll back the child. Look at his eyes.

HUMAYUN. Come! be brave. Ladies, I pray you raise your veils. Now, my son.

AKBAR. [*Pauses, hesitates, then like an arrow from a bow runs forward with the cry.*] Amma! Amma-jan!

BAIRAM KHAN. [*Aside.*] I backed the boy, and I will back him to the end.

—17—

AKBAR'S RESOLVE.

Akbar came to the throne at his father's death, when he was twelve years of age. Bairam Khan was his tutor and guardian and right well had he kept his promise of backing the little lad's fortunes. But he was domineering and arrogant, and from the very beginning his methods of government ran counter to those of the boy-king, who from the first realised the responsibilities of kingship far more keenly than any of his contemporaries in any part of the world. So at the early age of eighteen he dismissed his minister, and from that time ruled his people on entirely new lines and with a wisdom seldom equalled and never excelled.

DRAMATIS PERSONÆ.

AKBAR, Emperor of India.

BAIRAM KHAN, his Prime Minister and past guardian.

MAHAM ANAGAH, Akbar's foster-mother.

ADHAM KHAN, Akbar's foster-brother.

PIR MAHOMED KHAN, Akbar's old tutor.

CHAMBERLAIN.

SCENE.

A private room in a palace at Delhi.

[MAHAM ANAGAH *and* AKBAR *alone.*]

MAHAM. [*Weeping.*] After all these years that you should flout me, set my wits at naught—you whom I nursed and cherished as my own, nay more than that, more by a thousand times!

AKBAR. [*Gravely.*] My more than mother, canst not understand? A man can only do what seems him best, if—as you sure must wish—he sets the good of many as worth more than that of a few. Bairam hath been my friend but from the first. [*He shivers.*] Why, the mere memory disgusts me. After the battle when he brought to me—to me a boy of twelve, new come to kingship—that wretched Hemu, bleeding, wounded, ill, and bade me cut him down, giving me, as whet to such base deed, my father's sword: "Boy! prove your mettle on this infidel;" and when I said I would not, when I cried, "I strike no wounded man! I will not whet my kingly sword on aught but strength and sense," he took the sword, my father's sword, and cut him down himself. Ah! savage! brutal! infamous! Ever since then, kind though he is, sagacious in his way, I've felt him as a drag on what I dream. No! he must go. It is not that he sent without one reference to me the dear old Pir, my ancient tutor, to most unneeded banishment—it is because in every way he thwarts me in my dream of perfect tolerance.

MAHAM ANAGAH. [*Still whimpering.*] Ay, dreams and dreams and dreams! You did not get them from my milk, I'll swear.

AKBAR. [*Frowning.*] No! and that reminds me— [*Claps his hands; a servant appears.*] Bid Adham Khan come hither. [*The servant retires.*]

[AKBAR *turns to* MAHAM ANAGAH.] My more than mother, I would fain not hurt your kindly heart, but Adham is your son. So I will speak to him when you can hear each word I say, and know it is deserved.

[*Enter* ADHAM KHAN; *he salutes.*]

[*Continuing.*] Adham, I have a word to say to you. I say it in your mother's presence, fairly, squarely. You must not presume, because you are my foster-brother. From afar come tales of wanton wickedness, of reckless pride. My subjects are outraged, my people's peace disturbed. I will not have it. If these tales recur you shall be punished were you fifty times my foster-brother, and your mother there had done for me a thousand times what she has done—though that were beyond thought since she has left undone no single thing.

[*He takes* MAHAM ANAGAH'S *hands, raises them to his forehead and then gently conducts her to the door.*] [*Enter* CHAMBERLAIN.]

CHAMBERLAIN. Pir Mahomed Khan.

PIR MAHOMED. Most illustrious! hearing that for my sake you would dismiss Bairam, I come to beg you to consider. You are young; the times are difficult. His wisdom—

AKBAR. [*Smiling.*] I have some too, although you saw small trace of wit or wisdom in my schoolboy days. And Bairam has been dismissed already. The message that I sent him was writ fair—but not by me, my tutor. Never would I learn to be a scribe, as thou knowest well. I told him that till now my royal will had been that he should rule, but now my mind had changed; that it was my intention in future to control all things and by my judgment, unaided, uncontrolled, to govern as I chose. He did not take it well. He tried to breed dissension. He has failed. He sent last night to ask for mercy.

PIR MAHOMED. Most clement! thou wilt pardon. He meant well; he —

AKBAR. [*Interrupting.*] I sent at dawn a guard of honour, equal to mine own, to bring him hither with all dignity. Hark! he comes.

[*Enter guard of honour in charge of* BAIRAM]

[AKBAR *steps forward to meet the old Minister and salutes him deferentially and leads him to the place of honour.*]

BAIRAM. [*Falling at his feet.*] O King, most clement! you are King indeed. I am not worthy.

AKBAR. Tchut! no words of that. In this strange world all men must take their place and do their best, as best it seems to them. You have done well in that old world where might was everything and where each fellow had the right to clutch at what his sword would get for him. But to my eyes a fairer world unfolds, a world of peace and tolerance, where man and child and woman shall have right, equal and fair, to serve themselves and God, as best they can. So leave me to my dream, old friend! If thou shouldst wish a military life, be Governor of Kalpi: it should hold enough ambition for advancing years. But if the Court would better please thee, why then, favour and honour shall be his who lived for us and ours. Yet if he choose devotion he shall have escort worthy of his rank to Mecca's shrine with ample pension. Choose thou, then, old friend, but leave me to my dream!

—18—

THE FIRST FOOTHOLD.

Ralph Fitch, John Newbery and William Leedes were the first ambassadors from Great Britain to India. After many adventures by the way, they turned up about the beginning of the hot weather in the year 1585 at the great Akbar's Court at Agra, and delivered to him a letter from Queen Elizabeth of England addressed to "Yellabdin Echebar, King of Cambaya, Invincible Emperor." It asked only for safe conduct through the Empire; and this was granted.

DRAMATIS PERSONÆ.

AKBAR, the Great Mogul.
ABUL-FAZL, his Prime Minister.
BIRBAL, Akbar's great friend.
RALPH FITCH, a citizen and trader from London.
JOHN NEWBERY, a British trader from Aleppo.
WILLIAM LEEDES, an English jeweller.
A SCRIBE.
PURSE-BEARER.
Nobles, etc.

SCENE.

The Diwan-i-am at Akbar's Court at Agra. AKBAR *is on his throne, nobles and courtiers beside him, and in the centre, below the dais, stand three Englishmen travel-stained and worn. It is early morning.*

AKBAR. [*In a loud sonorous voice.*] Read the last portion of the Queen's letter once more.

ABUL-FAZL. "By the singular report of Your Majesty's humanity, we use the fewer and less words, and only request that these our subjects may be honestly treated and received. And that in respect of their hard journey it would please Your Majesty with some liberty and security of voyage to grant them such privileges as to you shall seem good."

AKBAR. Enough. Write down their names, scribe. [*Addressing the Englishmen and pointing to one.*] Your name, sir?

JOHN NEWBERY. John Newbery, of Aleppo.

AKBAR. Your purpose?

JOHN NEWBERY. Trade and travel.

AKBAR. [*Looking keenly at him.*] Ha! more of the latter than the former, I'll warrant me. But you, sir, are trader born.

RALPH FITCH. Ay, Sire, Ralph Fitch of London.

AKBAR. And you?

WILLIAM LEEDES. A jeweller. I cut gems like this, my Liege.

[*He draws from his bosom a large rose-cut diamond. The nobles press forward.* AKBAR *holds it between his finger and thumb. It flashes.*]]

AKBAR. Beautiful indeed! See, Abul, how many faces it has and each reflects the sun! It is like a perfect life. [*To* WILLIAM LEEDES.] You could cut such gems here?

WILLIAM LEEDES. Ay, my Liege.

RALPH FITCH. [*Eagerly.*] And we could bring India gold too.

AKBAR. [*Haughtily.*] We have no need of gold. Purse-bearer! bring forth the immortal money and show these strangers we need no gold.

PURSE-BEARER. My lord!

AKBAR. Read out the legends on the coins, Abul.

ABUL-FAZL. My Lord. Know, O strangers! this coin values one hundred of your pounds. And this is written:

"I am a golden coin,
May golden be its use."

On the other side this:

"Golden it is to help
The seeker after truth."

And this is worth fifty of your pounds. On it is written:

"God in His pleasure
Gives without measure."

JOHN NEWBERY. [*Readily.*] Enough. We ask but that, following this divine example, the mighty Yellabdin Echebar would grant our pleasure without measure.

AKBAR. What say you, Birbal?

BIRBAL. Wanderers are always beggars, Sire.

AKBAR. [*Quickly.*] My purse has pennies left for alms.

PURSE-BEARER. I like not the jewel business, Sire.

AKBAR. My crown can spare a gem or two. What say you, Abul-Fazl?

ABUL-FAZL. These men come, Sire, by their own showing, from a nation of traders. It were well ere granting liberty, to make them understand that our laws demand fair dealing from both seller and buyer.

[*The three Englishmen look at one another doubtfully.*]

RALPH FITCH. Our law is different, it leaves each free. But by the fame for justice of our Queen and of our country we engage to do naught unbecoming of either.

AKBAR. [*Sharply.*] And to abide by my laws?

JOHN NEWBERY. And to abide by the laws of this land. [*Aside.*] So long as they shall last.

AKBAR. Scribe, write out a *sunnud* of safety while they are in my realms. Who injures them is responsible to me. Gentlemen, you may go.

[*They make obeisance and go.*]

JOHN NEWBERY. [*Aside.*] We have gained a foothold; let others see that they keep it. I am more for travel and to see the world as the Great Mogul said. Lo! he has eyes to pierce through a man.

RALPH FITCH. Yea! the path is clear. Saw you ever such riches, such diamonds?

WILLIAM LEEDES. [*Dreamily.*] The one on his turban was as large as an egg. Yet, were it cut it would lose much.

RALPH FITCH. [*Joyously.*] And gain more! My masters, what tales shall we not have to tell when we return? How mouths will water and fingers itch to touch the untold wealth of India! [*He rubs his hands and laughs gleefully.*] But as we said, " Free, fair trade. Ay! free and fair."

—19—

JAHANGIR AND NURJAHAN.

The story of the Emperor Jahangir's love for the beautiful Persian Nurjahan is too well known to need re-telling. He saw her first at his father's court, but did not succeed in inducing her to marry him till twenty years had passed. He was then fast going downhill; drunken, dissolute, the end must have come soon. She, by her influence, restored him to some measure of dignity and self-control, and for sixteen years was practically joint-ruler with him of Hindostan. Many were the cabals against her, but she won her way through all, and confuted the critics who said her actions were the outcome of personal ambition, by retiring absolutely from public life at her husband's death, and living as a widow engaged solely in charitable works.

The story of how she once nearly lost her hold over the Emperor is told in the following playlet, which shows how Jahangir was kidnapped, held prisoner, induced to sign Nurjahan's death-warrant, and how the mere sight of her was sufficient to restore her ascendancy and confound the plotters.

DRAMATIS PERSONÆ.

JAHANGIR, Emperor of India.
NURJAHAN, his wife, Empress of India.
ASAF KHAN, Nurjahan's brother.
MAHABAT KHAN, Governor of Bengal and rebel.
BARKHURDAR, Mahabat's son.
FIDAI KHAN, an adherent of Nurjahan.
Nobles, Messengers, Cup-bearers, etc.

SCENE I.

A tent on the bank of the Jhelum river. It is late at night. JAHANGIR *reclines on a couch.* ASAF KHAN *sits beside him. Two or three other nobles form the group. They are all drinking.*

JAHANGIR. [*Raising his ruby cup.*] One more cup, gentlemen. What shall the toast be?

A NOBLEMAN. To the fair one's eyes!

JAHANGIR. [*Frowning*] Fool! thou art drunk indeed. Who cares for your mistress's eyes?

FIDAI KHAN. [*Holding up his goblet.*] May Heaven give long life to the Empress of India!

JAHANGIR. [*Mollified.*] Come, that is better. We will have another cup to that!

[*The cup-bearer fills the goblets.*]

MESSENGER. Sire! Her Highness the Empress of India craves audience and cannot wait, since it is past twelve of the clock.

JAHANGIR. [*Sleepily.*] I dreamed it not so late. Gentlemen, good-night. I must to my bed.

[*Exeunt* ASAF KHAN *and* NOBLES.]

ASAF KHAN. With your permission, Sire, I will remain and see my sister. I would have a word with her.

JAHANGIR. [*Solemnly; he is slightly the worse for drink.*] And with none better. She is marvellous, simply marvellous. Her wits—[*Shakes his head foolishly.*]

[*Enter* NURJAHAN; *she salaams in courtly fashion, then goes to stand beside Jahangir.*]

NURJAHAN. My lord, 'tis later than you thought, and fully time you rested from the duties of the day

To-morrow, too, will be most tiring. We must cross the river and that takes time. Ah! Asaf, is that you? What news of this Mahabat Khan?

ASAF KHAN. They say he lingers on our rear with more than fifteen thousand men, mostly Rajputs.

NURJAHAN. Traitor and rebel! He shall meet his match when once my lord is safe and well in Kabul. [*To* JAHANGIR.] Has the cough troubled much to-day, my lord?

JAHANGIR. Somewhat; it would be bettered by another glass.

NURJAHAN. Not after twelve, my lord; your wont is otherwise. See, I will call for your attendant.

[*Claps her hands. Servant enters.*]

May soundest sleep attend my lord, and pleasant dreams be his until the dawning of the day! [*She falls at the* EMPEROR'S *feet and kisses them. In a low voice.*] Your slave bids you good-night.

JAHANGIR. [*Leaning on his attendant's arm.*] There's but one woman in the world, my Queen. Good-night.

[*Exit.*]

NURJAHAN. [*Rising.*] That makes it worth the while! He's more a king when I can stand between him and his faults. Ah, Asaf! how I miss my father's shrewd old wit. I often think how well he shaped the course even from the time when those quaint Englishmen came asking grants for this and that. "See you, speak fair!" he said. "In times to come our India will owe much to these same merchant-men. We hoard our gold too close. They spend it and so make God's earth more fruitful." Ah! had I a free hand, I'd make this country learn a lesson.

ASAF. You have not taught Mahabat his as yet.

NURJAHAN. [*Frowning.*] No! but I will. He's backed, see you, by Khurram, once the one of all the Emperor's sons I favoured most. I thought him like great Akbar: but I trust him not; I think he killed his brother. Anyhow, I have to get the King safe into Kabul. The cool air, the joyous quiet life, will cure him of his asthma.

MESSENGER. Fidai Khan would fain have audience now.

NURJAHAN. Admit him. [*Messenger goes.*]

NURJAHAN. It must be of grave import, so late as this.

[*Enter* FIDAI KHAN. *He is accoutred for a march.*]

FIDAI KHAN. My lady liege, I crave to be allowed to keep my company this side the bridge, till daylight comes. I live it not the royal tents should stand so poor protected. If the word is given I'll halt my men who even now pass by to take position on the further side.

NURJAHAN. But whence this fear? Hast heard of any plot against my lord?

FIDAI KHAN. None! but devotion dreams of ill where none exists, mayhap.

NURJAHAN. Then 'tis devotion's part to give up dreams and do its duty. There is no fear, Fidai, thou best of friends.

FIDAI KHAN. So be it, lady.

[*Goes; bugles sound, tramping of feet outside.*]

NURJAHAN. [*Smiling.*] Poor Fidai! how often does he dream of ill to me, his mistress. Never was a servant so devoted. Well, good-night. God's blessing go with you.

[*Exeunt different sides ; lights are lowered.*]

[*A long pause. A gong sounds once, then twice, then three times. Three hours are supposed to elapse.*]

[*Suddenly the tent flap lifts, a man steals in.*]

[VOICE *from behind.*] Hush! man, hush! This must be done in silence.

[*Four or five men slip in, also* MAHABAT *and* BARKHURDAR.]

MAHABAT. [*In a whisper.*] The Emperor sleeps within; the guards are gagged and there remain but the two watchmen. Kasim, you take one, Rai Singh the other. Now, quiet as mice.

[*Exeunt to the sleeping tent within.*]

[*Faint sounds are heard.*]

MAHABAT. [*Coming in again. He holds one arm of the* EMPEROR *who is in his night garment,* BARKHURDAR *the other.*] My Liege, you are our prisoner.

JAHANGIR. [*But half awake.*] How? What? Where am I?

MAHABAT. In the hands of friends who fain would give you freedom.

JAHANGIR. Mahabat! is it thou, and this thy son?

BARKHURDAR. Whom thy Queen scourged with thorns and drove from court.

JAHANGIR. [*With a silly laugh.*] Come, that was I. Let's have fair play at least.

MAHABAT. [*Impatiently.*] Come! come! we must away.

JAHANGIR. Not as I am. [*Looks at his clothes.*] Let me at least go to the women's tents and put on decent clothes.

MAHABAT. What! to the women's tent? No, no! That were fresh slavery. Quick! bring my lord's dressing-gown and something warm to lap him in. Fear not, most mighty! We are your friends.

[*Exeunt hastily,* JAHANGIR *feebly protesting.*]

DRAMATIS PERSONÆ.

JAHANGIR.	MAHABAT.
NURJAHAN.	1ST MINISTER.
FIDAI KHAN	2ND MINISTER.

Nobles, Messengers, Cup-bearers, Acrobat, etc.

SCENE II.

A royal room; everything magnificent. Obsequious cup-bearers. JAHANGIR *reclining on a couch. A boy playing antics before him.* MAHABAT *looking on.*

JAHANGIR. Go away! I am tired.

[BOY *crestfallen goes.*]

Slaves, another cup of wine.

[*Holds out the ruby cup.*]

MAHABAT. What further does my lord desire? All that this country holds of joy or wealth is his and none dare say, "Forbear! forbear!"

JAHANGIR. [*Heaving a sigh.*] Yea! yea! I am free. [*Holds out the ruby cup.*] Another cup of wine —dost hear?

MAHABAT. [*Guilefully.*] Not yours alone, is freedom. All the country rings with joy that the arch mischief-maker 's gone. Yet 'twas not her fault that matters went awry. What else could one expect? She was but a woman!

JAHANGIR. True! I was a fool to trust her. [*To* CUP-BEARER.] Fill my cup again.

MAHABAT. No fool, my lord; your wisdom has no flaw. Given but freedom from a woman's guile you'd shine the wisest monarch upon earth.

JAHANGIR. [*Shaking his head.*] Most true! most true! I am but a fool where women are concerned.

MAHABAT. Say not so: where but one woman is concerned, my lord! That woman must be sent where she can do no mischief.

JAHANGIR. Exiled?

MAHABAT. Ay! to the Land of Death.

JAHANGIR. [*Feebly.*] Not that.

MAHABAT. Naught else will do. The Queen, as you have heard, has given herself up, being vanquished; but already cabal is rife, trouble will follow. It is not I alone but all your friends beseech you. Even now there waits below a deputation from your trusted Ministers. I will call them up. [*To* MESSENGER.] Go! bid the Ministers appear.

1ST MINISTER. Most mighty! we thy servants humbly pray to be set free for ever from the thrall of womanhood in matters far beyond the arts of woman. Sign this warrant of death and thy renown will rise beyond the realms of thought.

2ND MINISTER. Bethink thee, merciful! 'tis one against a million. One poor soul sent unto Paradise, a million men here on this earth at peace. The exchange is good, my King.

MAHABAT. Here is the paper; but a scratch and the thing 's done. Have courage, Jahangir. Thou didst not lack it when we charged the foe together in the olden days.

JAHANGIR. No, I'm no coward; here, the pen. [*Writes hurriedly, flings the pen away.*] Another cup of wine.

MAHABAT. [*Turning away aside.*] Go, give him ten! it matters not now he has signed. Go, give the warrant to the Commandant and bid him do his duty. Quick! [*Turning* to JAHANGIR *briskly.*] And now great King, to business. I have news of much importance. Rohtas is taken. Asaf Khan has retired to further shelter.

JAHANGIR. That is good.

MAHABAT. From the Deccan comes great news of great success. On every side is victory. Ere the year 's out, all India will admit Jahangir's rule. And wherefore not, since, as his name implies, he girds the world?

1ST MINISTER. Ay! so he will: not India, but the world. [*Enter* FIDAI KHAN.]

FIDAI KHAN. I come, O King! burdened with a request, from one you once held dear: not a request in truth, but a demand; a claim in short that cannot be denied. Queen Nurjahan, your wife, begs ere she dies—dies willingly, mark you, by your command—that she may once more kiss your feet. She bids me say that you could trust her not to make a scene.

[JAHANGIR *looks from one to the other dubiously.*]

MAHABAT. [*Quickly.*] Why should the King?

FIDAI KHAN. [*Quicker.*] She bade me beg you to seek counsel from your heart, my Liege, not from men's tongues.

[*A moment's pause.*]

JAHANGIR. [*In a broken voice.*] Bid her come. [*To the* MINISTERS.] It can do no harm.

MAHABAT. [*Concealing his vexation.*] No harm at all. Meanwhile let us proceed to business more important.

FIDAI KHAN. Nay! My mistress waits without. [*To* JAHANGIR.] Shall she come in, my Liege?

JAHANGIR. [*Weakly overcome. To himself.*] So close! [*Aloud.*] Ah, let her come.

[*Enter* NURJAHAN *closely veiled in white. She walks quietly to* JAHANGIR, *falls at his feet.*]

NURJAHAN. [*In a low voice.*] Good-night, my lord, good-night.

[*As she rises* JAHANGIR *catches at her hand and holds her fast.*]

JAHANGIR. [*In a loud voice.*] No! no! This shall not, must not be. I — I cannot — no, I will not!

NURJAHAN. [*Gently.*] If my lord wills my death, I die with joy; if life, I live to be his slave.

[*She stands proudly beside the* EMPEROR, *seeming to defy all present.*]

JAHANGIR. [*Still holding her hand.*] What can I say? Ah, men! she is my friend. I cannot let her go. Have pity on us both. I beg — I pray.

MAHABAT. It is not fer the Emperor of India to beg in vain.

[*Tears up the death-warrant; goes.*]

[*Exeunt all.*]

[MAHABAT, *as he goes.*] We must find some other way to clip the witch's wings.

[JAHANGIR *and* NURJAHAN *are left standing together. She lifts her veil and looks around.*]

NURJAHAN. Cup-bearer, take the wine away. My lord desires no more.

—20—

A SURGEON'S FEE.

Shahjahan was the most magnificent of Indian Emperors. In his time the wise inactions of his grandfather, the great Akbar, bore fruit, and he himself was wise enough not to interfere with the great scheme of Empire that Akbar started. He was therefore, rich beyond compare, and being of artistic intellectual nature, he spent his money in artistic ways. Amongst other beautiful buildings, the Taj stands supreme. It is a memorial to Arjumand Banu, Shahjahan's beloved wife, who bore him thirteen children. In later life Shahjahan was shamefully used by his sons and spent many years imprisoned in the palace at Agra. Here his devoted and much beloved companion was his daughter Padishah or Jahanara Begum. From the affection he lavished upon her we judge that she must have closely resembled her mother, the dead Arjumand.

DRAMATIS PERSONÆ.

SHAHJAHAN, Emperor of India.
LORD HIGH CHAMBERLAIN.
GABRIEL BOUGHTON, an English ship's surgeon.
1ST HAKIM.
2ND HAKIM.
MESSENGER.

SCENE.

A room in the palace at Agra. A balcony opens on to the curve of the river. The Taj is seen in the distance.

SHAHJAHAN. [*Alone walking up and down.*] Patience—so they bid me! patience, when my one ewe lamb, my only one, lies at death's door! Her brothers do not care: they keep me here a prisoner for their ends, and I—[*Goes to balcony.*] Ah Arjumand! dear Arjumand! you lie at peace. Your sons torment you not. [*Covers his face with his hands.*]

[*Enter* LORD HIGH CHAMBERLAIN.]

CHAMBERLAIN. My lord, this is not well. God will be merciful. He will save for you the sweetest lady ever the sun shone on.

SHAHJAHAN. No! not the sweetest. She lies there at rest. And yet—it seems so useless, friend—I cannot think. I seem to see the fire catch at her clothes. Oh! why was I not there to crush the fire out? Was there no man to fling his strength 'tween Death and those two helpless frightened girls?

CHAMBERLAIN. The Princess Jahanara did her best to save her friend. They were both dancing, Sire.

The flimsy robe caught in the lamp; the Princess, swift as thought, flung herself forward, caught the screaming girl, and so crushed the fire out. Too brave, alas! A cunning flame had touched her gauzy veil. It flared; the Princess, nothing daunted, tried to cast it off and did so; but the fire fled to her dress.

SHAHJAHAN. My poor, poor child!

CHAMBERLAIN. And there was none to help. The other women were not brave as she. Since then Your Majesty's physicians' skill has day and night been hers.

SHAHJAHAN. [*Feverishly.*] They bring no help. Day after day their faces lengthen. When, think you, will the Englishman be here? Their doctors have some brains; so may bring hope.

CHAMBERLAIN. Your message went post-haste, and he may come at any moment; for myself I deem their Western knowledge poor. I would rely —

SHAHJAHAN. [*Wringing his hands.*] It is a chance, man! Canst not understand, a drowning man will catch e'en at a straw? Ah! here come the doctors. What is your report?

1ST HAKIM. Your Highness must have patience. God will send recovery.

2ND HAKIM. Death, O Most Highest, brings to all men peace.

1ST HAKIM. She suffers not at all, that is one good.

SHAHJAHAN. [*Staggering.*] You mean — you cannot mean there is no hope!

1ST HAKIM. [*Echoing.*] No hope in mortal man, but God remains.

2ND HAKIM. Ay, He remains.

1ST HAKIM. And patience, Sire, patience!

SHAHJAHAN. Ah Jahanara! O my all! my link with the beloved past.

MESSENGER. Sire, the ship's doctor sent at your request from Surat has arrived.

SHAHJAHAN. Show him in here at once.

[*Enter* GABRIEL BOUGHTON *who bows.*]

GABRIEL. Sir, your servant. The case is urgent, I am told. I'd better see, without delay, the patient; and I pray there be no veilings; for such silly shams give Death advantage which he shall not have, with Gabriel Boughton.

SHAHJAHAN. Sir, you are welcome. [*To* HAKIMS.] Go with him, my friends, and on the way explain to him the treatment she has had.

GABRIEL. [*Bluntly.*] Sir! by your leave I'd rather go alone. My eyes are my best tutor and the wit of others may confuse them. Have I leave?

SHAHJAHAN. My Lord High Chamberlain, conduct him to the room where Princess Jahanara lies, and tell the tirewomen to do as he desires.

[*Exeunt* GABRIEL BOUGHTON *and* CHAMBERLAIN.]

1ST HAKIM. [*Offended.*] Sire! I take my leave. My service is not needed.

2ND HAKIM. Nor mine; so with your permission I retire.

SHAHJAHAN. [*Alone.*] Have I done right? To wound these learned men, outrage the laws which for long years have bound my women fast in strictest privacy! [*Passes to window.*] O Arjumand, my Queen, have I done right? She was as much your child as mine. Have I done right? It is at least a chance. [*Falls on his knees.*] [*Re-enter* GABRIEL BOUGHTON.] [SHAHJAHAN *starts up and comes hastily towards him.*]

GABRIEL. The girl will live, Your Highness, if she gets no more ginger and such filth. She suffers from the shock and must have beef-tea, brandy, milk. I saw her take the brandy and she seemed better at once. In fact, with decent care, she should do well.

SHAHJAHAN. [*Overcome.*] With—decent—care. [*Bursts out.*] Sir, you have put new life into my veins. You've raised a weight of care from my bent shoulders. What can I give you in return? Ask all I have to give and you shall have it. Naught in my realms that I can give shall be denied to you.

GABRIEL. [*Simply.*] Sir, I'm very glad to be of this small service. All the way your embassy has fed me like a prince, treated me like a king. Will doubtless do the same on my way back. Therefore I ask no more than common surgeon's fee—a gold *mohur.*

SHAHJAHAN. One golden *mohur* for bringing Hope from Heaven! Nay, good sir, you must ask more.

GABRIEL. [*Laughing.*] More than a *mohur*? [*Becomes serious.*] Yea! I will. I ask Your Majesty for what means nothing to myself, but much to those who work for England's empire in the world. Give them, O King, the right to trade without restriction through the length and breadth of Hindustan.

SHAHJAHAN. I grant it. [*Calls.*] Here! Send for a scribe at once; the *sunnud* shall be duly signed and sealed without delay.

GABRIEL. I thank Your Majesty, though I doubt me much, if in the future any one will know that England gained her first real footing in this land because a poor ship's surgeon asked for this as his fee. And now, great King, I go to see my patient and nurse her back to life.

—21—

SIVAJI'S STRATAGEM.

Sivaji, the great Maratha chief with whom began the rule of the Maratha power in India, was a fair match for Aurangzeb in artfulness and cunning. More than once he fairly outwitted the Mahomedan Emperor, and the story of one of his exploits as related below, gives a good idea of the sort of man he was, gay, reckless, unscrupulous, with a perfect genius for conspiracy. He was a little bit of a man, so his plan of escaping in a large basket was quite feasible.

DRAMATIS PERSONÆ.

SIVAJI, the Maratha chief.
SAMBHAJI, his son, five years old.
HINDU PHYSICIAN, in reality Sivaji's confederate.
MAHOMEDAN PHYSICIAN.
RANJI, BHANJI } Sivaji's confidential servants.
AURANGZEB, the Mogul Emperor.
A JAILER.

SCENE.

A prison. Sivaji, apparently very ill, lying on a truckle-bed. His little son Sambhaji is playing beside him; a Hindu jogi and a Mahomedan fakir sit motionless in the corner. Two very large baskets stand between them.

[HINDU PHYSICIAN *entering with the* MAHOMEDAN.]

HINDU PHYSICIAN. Possibly he is conscious, possibly not. He varies much.

SIVAJI. [*Muttering.*] Never again shall I see the blue hills of my beloved coast country. Never again shall I ride my charger along the rocky path that leads to Partabgarh. I am worse to-day than I was yesterday. I shall be worse to-morrow than I am to-day. There is nothing left but to die.

HINDU PHYSICIAN. Poor fellow! He seems almost at the last gasp.

MAHOMEDAN PHYSICIAN. Yet his voice is strong.

HINDU PHYSICIAN. [*Evasively*] That often occurs just before the end. [*Addressing the patient.*] My lord! this is the Mahomedan physician the Emperor Aurangzeb has sent to enquire after your health.

SIVAJI. [*Very faintly.*] He is — welcome. But it is no good. I have given alms and sweetmeats to every Hindu jogi and Mahomedan fakir. They all pray for me but — I am doomed!

MAHOMEDAN PHYSICIAN. [*Feeling the pulse.*] Say not so, my friend, your pulse is still quite strong.

HINDU PHYSICIAN. [*Hastily.*] That is an evil sign, I fear. But half an hour ago it trembled as if at death's door. I like not these unsteadinesses.

MAHOMEDAN PHYSICIAN. And his eye is bright.

HINDU PHYSICIAN. Ay! with fever.

MAHOMEDAN PHYSICIAN. He feels not hot to my touch.

HINDU PHYSICIAN. [*Superciliously.*] Likely not. But there are internal as well as external fevers.

MAHOMEDAN PHYSICIAN. [*Offended.*] I do not need the telling.

HINDU PHYSICIAN. [*Flattering.*] How should you when I learnt it from your most admirable treatise?

MAHOMEDAN PHYSICIAN. [*Flattered.*] Ah! so you have read my poor effort. Now, tell me, has the patient any other symptom of danger?

HINDU PHYSICIAN. [*Taken aback.*] I—I am not sure — I think — er —

SIVAJI. [*In a hollow voice.*] Doctor, I — I have not spoken of it — I — I know its import too well; but — but — since yesterday I have noticed a black spot over — my heart.

BOTH PHYSICIANS. [*Surprised.*] A black spot!

[*They look at each other.*]

Hum, indeed! A black spot! [*They proceed to examine the mark and shake their heads.*]

MAHOMEDAN PHYSICIAN. What it is I do not quite diagnose; but that it is serious. [*Shakes his head.*]

HINDU PHYSICIAN. I fear, very serious.

MAHOMEDAN PHYSICIAN. Well, I will go to the Emperor and tell him that the patient's condition will not admit of a personal interview with him.

SIVAJI. [*In a hollow voice.*] I want to say good-bye.

MAHOMEDAN PHYSICIAN. I trust, not so bad as that, my friend. [*As he goes out, he notices the baskets.*] Surely they are large.

HINDU PHYSICIAN. Very large; but every day my patient has increased his offerings. See! there wait the jogi and the fakir ready to distribute them. But up till now it has been of no use whatever. [*Sighs.*]

[*Exit* MAHOMEDAN PHYSICIAN.]

[*The instant he is out of the room* SIVAJI *jumps out of bed, laughing.*]

SIVAJI. The black mark did you both, and I've had it since I was born! So far good. Now to business. Is all prepared, Ranji?

RANJI. [*Rising.*] All, my lord, so far as the city gates. We need the pass.

SIVAJI. That will come. How! are those the baskets?

BHANJI. The largest we could get, my lord.

SIVAJI. Small enough. They're full of sweets, of course?

RANJI. No, my lord.

SIVAJI. No! fool. I bet my life Aurangzeb looks in. Quick! stuff them full of — anything. So: a kerchief, now those few sweets on the top. Put them in that dark corner where the light is bad. Now Sambhaji on to the bed. My child's eyes dance too much with thoughts of escape. Remember not one word, sonling.

SAMBHAJI. Not one word, father. Ah, isn't it fun?

SIVAJI. H'm! I think you had better pretend to sleep. So: your face buried in the quilt. Now for it. [*Gets into bed.*]

A JAILER. [*Opening door.*] I hear the Emperor approach. [*Exit.*]

HINDU PHYSICIAN. [*Solemnly.*] It is well: so does the end!

SIVAJI. [*In a whisper.*] Bravo! doctor. My end does — to-morrow I shall be in Muttra.

[*Enter* AURANGZEB. *He is very dignified and sanctimonious, but his cunning eyes are everywhere.*]

AURANGZEB. [*After looking at* SIVAJI *for some time.*] Can he not speak?

HINDU PHYSICIAN. At times, Most Noble! [*Steps to bed.*] My lord! the Emperor is here.

SIVAJI. [*Faintly.*] Nay! doctor, no more medicine.

'Tis useless. Why does the Emperor not come? I cannot die in peace.

AURANGZEB. The Emperor is here. What dost thou want of me?

SIVAJI. [*Trying to salute; then laying his hand on* SAMBHAJI.] This child, out-wearied with grief, he is no foe of thine. Let him go hence when I am gone.

AURANGZEB. Whither?

SIVAJI. To his mother at Muttra. 'Tis a last request, great foe; but Death — makes — all — folks — friends. [*Seems exhausted.*]

AURANGZEB. A goodly sentiment. It shall be as you desire.

SIVAJI. [*Faintly.*] But the paper, the pass. I want it now; I cannot die in peace without it: as Aurangzeb would have all men die.

AURANGZEB. [*To* PHYSICIAN.] What does he mean?

HINDU PHYSICIAN. He has been wandering, Most Mighty, and hath had a paper prepared. This is it, Most Excellent. [*Hands paper.*]

AURANGZEB. A pass to Muttra for the child and one Ranji, a jogi?

HINDU PHYSICIAN. He sits yonder.

[RANJI *rises and salaams.*]

AURANGZEB. [*Aside.*] What does this mean? I must consider. Meanwhile [*Draws off his ring*] bring ink, slaves. [*He stamps and returns paper, then stepping to the bed says meaningly.*] Thou hast thy wish, old foe. See that it brings no harm. [*Goes. As he is going his eye catches the baskets.*] What are those? [*Walks up to them.*]

HINDU PHYSICIAN. The offerings of sweets which by permission are sent.

AURANGZEB. [*Sardonically.*] The amount should have been more successful. Let me see inside.

[*The covers are removed.*]

[*Aside.*] H'm! There is something I do not understand. But [*Looks at* SIVAJI.] for to-night all is safe.

[*Exit.*]

SIVAJI. [*Jumping out of bed.*] Quick! He will double the guards and give orders to stop the gates. Quick! Your clothes, Ranji. [*Tears off his own.*] Into the basket, Sambhaji! Put the bag of rupees in to balance it. [*Hurriedly turning out sweets, etc.*] A kerchief on the top, some sweets; so, that will do. Now for myself. Stay! [*Runs to bed, seizes quilt, rolls it up into a dummy, claps his puggree on the top, arranges all with wonderful dexterity.*] So! that will deceive them for a while. Now, Sivaji for smallness. Ye gods, what a tight fit! No room for sweets. Ranji, are you ready?

RANJI. Ready, my lord.

[*Takes up the basket and trots out.*]

HINDU PHYSICIAN. [*At the door.*] Farewell! Good luck.

SIVAJI. [*From within the basket.*] We meet to-morrow at Muttra. [*A pause and silence.*]

HINDU PHYSICIAN. He has passed the prison guards by now: so far all is well.

[*Blows out lamp and exit.*]

[*Another pause.*]

[*Someone with a light opens the door gently and steals to bed. He is followed at a distance by another.*]

A MUFFLED VOICE. He is there in his bed, alive or dead. Send word to the Emperor, all is well this first hour.

— 22 —

A TYRANT'S DEATH-BED.

Although a very clever man, Aurangzeb undoubtedly caused the destruction of the Moghul Empire. Jahangir began it by flouting the great Akbar's scheme of religious unity and restoring the Mahomedan formula of faith to the coins of the realm. Aurangzed continued it, with the result that the monarchs who came after him can scarcely be called the Great Moghuls. Aurangzeb was a despot and a tyrant of the first water and the incident most worthy of chronicle in his reign is his death-bed, which gives, in all its horror, the picture of a dying man beset by remorse for the evil deeds he has done. Yet he always affected piety.

What was really the matter with him was this. He had no heart. The only person of whom he was fond was himself.

DRAMATIS PERSONÆ.

AURANGZEB, Emperor of India.
ROSHANARA, his sister.
A DOCTOR.
A SCRIBE.

Attendants.

SCENE.

A verandah room. A bed set with silken coverlets. A singing bird in a cage. It is night.

AURANGZEB. [*From his bed wearily.*] What time of the night is it?

ATTENDANT. Nigh dawn, my lord.

AURANGZEB. Will the night never end? Scribe, bring out the folios of my many letters.

SCRIBE. [*Bringing out a great pile of half-bound volumes.*] They are here, my lord. Which does Your Majesty require?

AURANGZEB. [*Restlessly.*] Which? Who knows! They are all the records of me. And I — [*More feebly*] Old age has arrived. The instant which has passed in power has left only sorrow behind it; ay! and fear, fear of my actions. [*Speaks louder.*] Still, come what may, I have launched my vessel on the waves. God knows I have worked hard; I never spared myself. And I built the mosque at Lahore in memory of Dara. I had to kill him — kill my brother: he was in the way; and those others. I did it for the best. Built with blood-money, blood-money! [*Enter the* DOCTOR.]

DOCTOR. [*Seriously.*] If the Most High thus distresses himself, he will do himself much harm.

AURANGZEB. What harm? Am I not dying? Do I not know it? Do I not feel it? And I have left so many things undone! Ah! if I had a few more years of life.

DOCTOR. [*Sanctimoniously.*] Most of us, Most Noble, feel there are things we would rather have left undone.

AURANGZEB. [*With sudden fierceness.*] Not I! I would do it all again; and more — and more. [*Relapses into quiet.*]

DOCTOR. He may sleep now. Let him be; medicines are of no use. [*Exit.*]

[*Enter* PRINCESS ROSHANARA.]

[AURANGZEB *stirs. She stands and looks at him.*]

ROSHANARA. Will he wake, I wonder? And to what? Poor miserable old man! Was it for this I sat beside him all those days guarding the Great Seal for him when, long ago, he was so ill? How changed from what he was in those old days! No! I dare not think of them. The shades of Dara, of Murad Bakhsh and Shuja—all my brothers, too!—rise up and mock me; yet I loved Aurangzeb best of them all. For his sake I said no word to stop his treatment of our father. For his sake—I—

AURANGZEB. [*Wakes.*] Who and what are you?

ROSHANARA. Thy sister, brother; she who sat beside you when long years ago you lay helpless and speechless; she who held for you the Seal of Office lest your foes should wrench it from your helpless hands.

AURANGZEB. I have forgotten. [*To Attendants.*] Take that bird away. Its gilded cage reminds me of my father whom I prisoned. But he deserved it; and then I was young and strong and he was old; but now I am old too! But he deserved his fate; and I his son—his son. [*A pause.*] I too have a son—nay! sons such as he had; but they will not work as I have; and I have worked so hard, so hard. We plotted; we planned. [*Long pause.*] Scribe! paper, ink. I will write a letter to my son, to—to Azam. In my will I've left him little. A letter may be useful: keep him quiet mayhap. [*Dictates.*]

"Son, nearest my heart. The agonies of death come upon me. I am going. Whatever good or evil I have done, it was done for you. Farewell! farewell! farewell!"

ROSHANARA. He sleeps again, and sleep stifles remorse: but only for a time, only for a time.

[*Goes weeping.*]

— 23 —

CALICO.

In 1498, just four years after the Emperor Babur came to the throne of Ferghana, an event occurred which was to change the whole future of India. One Vasco da Gama, a Portuguese master-mariner of good family, succeeded in reaching the town of Calicut on the western shores of India. He was led to the dangerous adventure of trying to cross the Indian Ocean by the sight, somewhere on the east coast of Africa, of two webs of cotton cloth which the owners said had been made in a land over-seas, "a land where there were all sorts of spices and precious stones, a land with all the riches of the world." This was the beginning of Western trade in India.

DRAMATIS PERSONÆ.

VASCO DA GAMA, Portuguese adventurer and mariner.
DIAZ, his mate.
1ST AFRICAN CHIEF.
2ND AFRICAN CHIEF.
PEDRO, a sailor.
Sailors, Natives.

DIAZ. [*Blowing his whistle.*] Pipe down the sails; and you, Pedro, see to the anchor. The Captain will rest the night nigh the river's mouth.

[*Whistling and* Yoh-ho-ho. *From outside enter* PEDRO.]

PEDRO. They lose no time on the shore, master. There be two boat-loads of the savages on their way already; but I can see no arms.

DIAZ. Nathless 'tis as well to be ready. Call up the guards, Pedro, and bid them bring their matchlocks.

[*Exit* PEDRO.]

[*Enter* VASCO DA GAMA, *a very handsome man with large dreamy eyes.*]

VASCO DA GAMA. [*To himself.*] So! anchored once more. The coast of this great continent seems endless, and as the good ship takes it, bay by bay, point by point, the compass shows ever due North. And I would go East. [*Scans the horizon.*] Nothing but sea, wide sea. Does land lie over there, I wonder? Ho! Diaz, any news?

DIAZ. Two boat-loads of natives, unarmed, approach. Your orders, please. I have sent for the matchlock-men.

VASCO DA GAMA. [*Quickly.*] Send them back again. How often do I tell thee, Diaz, that we are here not for bloodshed but for commerce.

DIAZ. [*Doggedly.*] Mayhap the one will not come without the other.

VASCO DA GAMA. Then will I neither! Lower the ladder, see you, and bring them hither with all honour.

DIAZ. Ay, ay, sir!

[*Exit.*]

VASCO DA GAMA. Shall I gain aught from these ignorant folks? God knows. Yet there must be something over yonder. [*Looks eastwards.*]

[*Enter* DIAZ, *escorting two* AFRICAN CHIEFS, *very stately and dignified.* PEDRO *follows with natives bearing baskets of fruits. The visitors seat themselves in reply to signs.*]

VASCO DA GAMA. [*Politely.*] Gentlemen, you are welcome. Now I wonder if they speak the same language as they do at Sofala! Pedro, try them. You know a word or two of the lingo.

PEDRO. I know how to ask for a drink.

1ST AFRICAN CHIEF. [*Solemnly.*] I speak little Portugee.

VASCO DA GAMA. Heaven be praised! Now I may get something. Ahem! Noble Chief. Much pleased. Diaz, bring a pistol. I will give him one. Nothing like fire-arms to unloose a savage's tongue. And see, put an apple on the hatch yonder.

[*He gesticulates to* CHIEFS *who watch with great interest.*]

See—pistol—that apple—shoot—so! [*Apple falls.*]

[*Amid confused murmurings of wonder* VASCO DA GAMA *rises and presents pistol to* CHIEF. *The two* CHIEFS *confer a moment, then signing to their followers produce the baskets of fruits and one containing two webs of fine calico.* 1ST AFRICAN CHIEF *puts latter at* DA GAMA'S *feet and makes sign it is in exchange for pistol.*]

2ND AFRICAN CHIEF. T'ank you, t'ank you, t'ank you.

VASCO DA GAMA. [*Curiously.*] What have we here? Saw I never the like! The stuff is soft as silk, yet 'tis not silk!

DIAZ. [*Leaning to look.*] Nay, 'tis not silk. God knows what 'tis.

1ST AFRICAN CHIEF. [*Smiling.*] Calico, calico.

[*The* SAILORS *laugh and echo* 'Calico, calico.']

VASCO DA GAMA. Calico, calico. But where is it made?

2nd AFRICAN CHIEF. Calicut, Calicut.

[*The* SAILORS *laugh and echo* 'Calicut, Calicut.']

VASCO DA GAMA. [*Laughing.*] Calicut, Calicut. Where is Calicut?

1ST AFRICAN CHIEF. [*Rising and pointing eastward.*] There.

VASCO DA GAMA. [*Starting up.*] There? Over the sea? [CHIEF *nods*] They make it? [CHIEF *nods.*] Big country? [CHIEF *signs to show bigness*] Rich? [CHIEF *touches his gold earrings and signs to show great wealth.*] Very far? [CHIEF *signs not so very far.*]

[VASCO DA GAMA *flings out his arms.*] At last! at last! Ho! you there Pedro, up with the anchor, and Diaz, pipe all hands to the sails. But stay; ere we start —[*He strides to the figure head of the Virgin, doffs his cap and kneels.*] all thanks to thee, most Holy Mary. Guide us, we pray thee, as thou hast guided us so far on this most perilous adventure. [*Rises, faces about.*] So now for the East! Farewell, good chiefs. Someone see them to their boats. Diaz, is the anchor up?

DIAZ. Ay, ay, sir!

VASCO DA GAMA. Then set her on her course due East, due East!

— 24 —

THE COLUMN OF DUPLEIX.

If the eyes of England had been on India with a view to trade with her, so had the eyes of France. As had been the case in England one company of merchants after another had been formed for the purpose of exploiting the East, until in A. D. 1719 some of the older companies joined together and business began in real earnest. Thenceforward the rivalry between the French and the English grew, and became acute in 1741 when the French appointed as Governor one Joseph Dupleix. They were lucky in their choice, for he was an extraordinarily able man. To begin with he had spent all his life in India where he had amassed a huge fortune. He was thus well acquainted with the manners and customs of the East, and his wife, a very clever woman who helped him in all his work, had been born and bred in India. The next ten years therefore were one long record of plots and counterplots in which the French had a decided advantage over the English, until one Robert Clive appeared on the side of the latter. He was quite a young man, but success went with him everywhere, and after a series of sieges, engagements and intrigues he completely broke the French power in India. As a sort of proof that he had done this, he utterly destroyed the memorial column which Dupleix had erected to celebrate his victories.

DRAMATIS PERSONÆ.

ROBERT CLIVE.
A CAPTAIN.
A SERGEANT.

MUBARAK }
BAHADUR } *Servants of Nasir Jang, the Nizam-ul-Mulk of the Deccan, who had been assassinated by order of Dupleix.*

1ST CITIZEN.
2ND CITIZEN.

Soldiers.

SCENE.

The City of Dupleix-Fathabad (or the City of Dupleix's Victory). The market-place; in the centre a column of four sides with an inscription on each in English, French, Persian and Tamil.

[*The* SERVANTS *of Nasir Jang and the* CITIZENS *are seated smoking and talking.*]

1ST CITIZEN. It is a fine tower.

MUBARAK. Mayhap, but it was built with blood-money. My master lost his life close to here by foulest assassination.

2ND CITIZEN. Call you it that? He was at the head of his army, and they say he commanded 300,000 soldiers.

BAHADUR. And if he did, what then? I am naught but a blunt soldier, but I hold that to sign a treaty one day and attack without warning the next is not fair play.

MUBARAK. That it was not; and who knows but the French were behind the Nawab of Kurnool who did the deed. Lo! I see it now, my master rising in his howdah to salute the Nawab. It was a foul deed.

1ST CITIZEN. Mayhap, but the English do not play fair always, though they do say there is a Captain-Sahib called Clive —

MUBARAK. Yea! yea! he is a tiger amongst men. My cousin is servant to him and tells many a tale. He fought with another Sahib not long since over cards. He said the other cheated. Then Clive Sahib's pistol snapped and the other holding his to the lad's head bade him beg for life. And he did.

1ST CITIZEN. He did? Lo! that was not brave.

BAHADUR. Hark to the end.

MUBARAK. So the fellow gave it him. But when demand was made that the accusation should be withdrawn Clive Sahib said coolly: "Not I! I said you cheated, and you did." So you see he held himself cheaper than the truth.

2ND CITIZEN. Well, he is fortunate in war. The runners brought news of a new victory to-day to the north over the French. Not that I care. One master is as good as another, so they leave us alone in peace — as they will.

BAHADUR. But Clive Sahib may come here.

1ST CITIZEN. Not he. 'Tis miles out of his way. He goes to Arcot.

[*Bugle sounds.*]

2ND CITIZEN. [*Jumping up.*] What's that?

A VOICE. [*Outside.*] Halt! Mark time till the main body forms up.

BAHADUR. Soldiers! Which side, I wonder?

MUBARAK. English. 'Tis all the English now!

BAHADUR. [*Running off.*] I'm for either side so long as there is fair fighting.

[MUBARAK *follows him.*]

MUBARAK. [*As he runs off.*] I am for fighting both sides.

1ST CITIZEN. Hai! Hai! War is upon us once more. Will it never end?

2ND CITIZEN. Hai! Hai! Why can the strangers not leave us in peace?

[*Enter* CLIVE *followed by his* CAPTAIN, SERGEANT *and four* SOLDIERS. *The* CITIZENS *salaam. He returns the salute but looks straight ahead.*]

CLIVE. So that's the column, the column of victory which Monsieur Dupleix has thought fit to erect. Ha! ha! Sergeant, go prod it with your bayonet. Tell me of what it is made.

SERGEANT. Yes, sir. [*Marches his four off.*]

CLIVE. No Englishman could ever have built a thing like that.

CAPTAIN. No, sir; and on the very place where he was party to a foul murder! for it was just here — wasn't it, sir? — that the Nizam-ul-Mulk was shot.

CLIVE. That is a trifle. It is the bombast of it, the intolerable arrogance. Pah! it makes me sick. Well, Sergeant.

[SERGEANT *re-enters.*]

SERGEANT. *Pukka chunam* outside, sir, muck in.

CLIVE. Most appropriate! It will be muck. [*To* CAPTAIN.] Bring your company up, sir, and bid Captain Green bring his pioneers.

CAPTAIN. [*Saluting.*] Sir. [*Goes out.*]

CLIVE. [*Addressing* CITIZENS.] No you shall see what that fox Dupleix's victories are worth. Look at them blazoned up there in four languages. I am only going to use one for mine. Dust and ashes! Are you all formed up over there? [*Speaks loud and looking straight ahead of him.*] Now men, we have by the grace of God and the valour of our arms beaten the French off the field. They have not one leg left upon which they can stand. And we are not going to allow this column, inscribed with all their so-called victories, to have one either. Pioneers forward! Hatchets and picks! I have marched you twenty miles out of your way on purpose for this affair, so my whole army may join in if it chooses.

[*A roaring cheer; sounds of falling bricks, mortar. General hubbub.*]

[CLIVE *listens a moment, a smile on his face.*]

They enjoy their task. It is a regular game to them; and it ends the game of the French and English once and for ever. So now to get some breakfast. [*Exit.*]

[*Noise continues, finally silence; then a chorus of "God save the King" from behind the scene.*]

— 25 —

CLIVE.

No one who reads Indian History but knows this name. From the day on which a lad of eighteen, taciturn and dogged, he entered India as a writer in the East India Company's service to that on which, out-wearied by the intolerable injustice of those whose greed of gold he had striven so hard to curb, he ended his life by an over-dose of opium, his great personality dominated the whole of India. His isolated acts may not all be unimpeachable, but he forced the eyes of England from the low standard of gold to the higher one of Empire; forced her to take up the burden of righteous administration, which to-day is the glory alike of mighty India and the Empire of which she forms a part.

DRAMATIS PERSONÆ.

ROBERT CLIVE.
CAPTAIN EYRE COOTE, afterwards Sir Eyre Coote.
MAJOR KILPATRICK, in command of a detachment.
A MESSENGER from Mir Jafar.
1ST ORDERLY OFFICER.
2ND ORDERLY OFFICER.

SCENE.

The field of Plassey. The roof of a hunting-box on the bank of the river Ganges, close to a large mango grove. A table littered with papers; two chairs.

[ROBERT CLIVE *looking out over the mango grove, and the vast semi-circle of the Nawab's troops hemming him in on all sides save the river.*]

CLIVE. I admit it is a great risk. But what will you? "Give naught gain naught," is a sound proverb.

CAPTAIN COOTE. You know I am against you, sir.

CLIVE. Well, you need not be so intolerably dismal about it, Coote. The council of war was in my favour.

COOTE: By loading the dice, sir. You gave your opinion first, instead of last as usual. The majority could not choose but follow Sabat Jung, as the sepoys call you.

CLIVE. [*Musing.*] "Daring in War," eh? Not a bad name in this country where audacity counts for so much. Yet your arguments nearly shook me, Coote. I spent two hours of solitary thought over them afterwards before I accepted the risk.

COOTE. A great risk. Siraj-ud-daula has 50,000 infantry, near 18,000 cavalry and 50 guns against our force of 3,000 all told.

CLIVE. [*Drily.*] Excuse me. He has more. You have forgotten the Frenchman Sinfray and his contingent. It is as well to be accurate when one is counting up one's enemies. [*Smiles suddenly.*] But it has to be, Coote, it has to be. If Siraj-ud-daula was a real man — even such a man as the peasants are about here—I might hesitate before attacking; but the young man is a simple brute, a monster hoary in vice; and he will topple over like a house of cards, at the first touch, I assure you. And then, look you, Coote! I have other work to do when this is over. I have to settle England's hold on India on decent and honourable lines. I have to clean the Augean stable of the services. Even the army, Coote, is not immaculate.

COOTE. [*Huffily.*] I fail to see, sir, that we are any worse.

CLIVE. Worse? Good Heavens! no, that is impossible. Why! there is hardly one official high or low, but has his fingers in the purse of some petty rajah or another. And that must be stopped if we are to hold India. And we must. So to-day decides it. If I hold over till to-morrow, Mir Jafar, the Nawab's uncle, who only waits to see which side the cat will jump, will decide against us. He is absolutely untrustworthy ; but if we win he can be bribed to do his duty. Omichand is hopeless — also absolutely faithless. I consider him the biggest rascal in the world. Yet I must play with him too! [*Walks about restlessly.*] But of that by and by. Meanwhile I so far fall in with your caution, that I will not attack till nightfall. That will hide the smallness of our force. So, now to rest.

COOTE. Good-bye, sir, and I wish I were as confident as you.

CLIVE. Confident? Good Heavens! sir, who can be confident when they risk all on the hazard of a die? I hope: that is all.

[*Exit* COOTE.]

[CLIVE, *looking out over the massed enemy.*] If this miscarries all the blame will be laid on me, not on the fools who have brought about the *impasse.* Well, so be it.

[*Lays himself on a couch and falls asleep in a second.*]

[*Enter* MAJOR KILPATRICK *in a hurry.*]

KILPATRICK. Sir, sir.

CLIVE. [*Yawning.*] Well, what is it?

KILPATRICK. The enemy is retiring — why, God knows! — without the exchange of a shot. Seizing the opportunity, I have ordered an attack on the tank occupied by the French.

CLIVE. [*Starting.*] *You* have ordered! What the devil do you mean by acting on your own responsibility, sir? I'll have you cashiered. It must be stopped at once. There is to be no attack till nightfall.

[*Rushes out followed by* MAJOR KILPATRICK.]

[*A pause, desultory firing, shouts, etc.*]

[*Re-enter* CLIVE.]

[*To himself.*] Kilpatrick was right. The opportunity had come. Yes! he was right. He has brains. I must remember him. [*Buckles on his sword.*] So now for the cast of the die: victory or defeat before sunset.

[*Enter* 1ST ORDERLY OFFICER.]

1ST ORDERLY OFFICER. The tank is taken, sir; but a large section of the enemy is detaching itself to the south-east and is advancing against us.

CLIVE. Tell Captain Coote to send a detachment to oppose it at once. I will be there myself in a few moments.

[*Hurriedly puts paper together on table, looks for a second or two at the map.*]

[*Enter* 2ND ORDERLY OFFICER.]

2ND ORDERLY OFFICER. The advancing troops, sir, appear to be friends. Mir Jafar is at their head.

CLIVE. [*Bursting into a laugh.*] Mir Jafar? Prince of rats! The ship must be sinking indeed or he would not leave it. So, let me think. Yes, send orders for general attack all along the line. Now is our chance. We must push it home.

[*Re-enter* 1ST ORDERLY OFFICER.]

[CLIVE *sits down at the table, writes hurried orders and hands them to the two* ORDERLY OFFICERS *who exeunt hurriedly.*]

[CLIVE, *still sitting and biting his nails.*]

Why did the enemy retire? Is it possible that it is a trick? No, for Mir Jafar—

[*Re-enter* 2ND ORDERLY OFFICER.]

2ND ORDERLY OFFICER. This man, sir, brings a message from—

MESSENGER. Mir Jafar Sahib Bahadur.

[*Presents a letter.*]

CLIVE. [*Tears letter open and reads, then flings it aside.*] The double-dyed traitor! Upon my soul I feel for the first time in my life some pity for that miserable villain of a Nawab. To have such men about him! Scoundrels who can advise a general retirement, then send secret letters counselling attack to the enemy. By Heavens! I will have my revenge on them when the time comes. But that is not yet—not yet! England comes first. 'Tis only the first part of her victory that has been won at the field of Plassey. The rest remains for other hands, and yet other hands than mine to do. And it will be done.

— 26 —

PRINCESS KRISHNA KUMARI.

While the Europeans were founding settlements on India's coral strand, the central portions of the great peninsula remained quite untouched by Western influence. Rajputana especially held to its old traditions, so that it was possible for the following incident to occur so late as the beginning of the nineteenth century, when the coast line of India was fairly civilized. Yet even here Rana Bhim's action shows that the fine old Rajput's creed of "Honour before Life" was weakening.

DRAMATIS PERSONÆ.

BHIM SINGH, Rana of Udaipur.
AMBASSADOR from Jaipur.
AMBASSADOR from Sindhia.
PRINCESS KRISHNA KUMARI, Bhim Singh's daughter.
HER MOTHER, Bhim Singh's wife.
HER BROTHER, Bhim Singh's son.
SAGWANT SINGH, Chief of Karradur.
Attendants, Chamberlain, etc.

SCENE.

The private audience-hall at Chitor, the chief town of Udaipur.

BHIM SINGH. [*On his throne.*] But I am bound by my word to my cousin of Jaipur.

JAIPUR'S AMBASSADOR. Ay! and I claim fulfilment. The Princess Krishna Kumari must be forthwith wedded to my master, or instant war will follow to avenge the insult.

SINDHIA'S AMBASSADOR. And if my master's request — nay! seeing that he is overlord, his *order* be not acted upon, his armies will soon enforce it. She must marry the Rajah of Jodhpur.

BHIM SINGH. In either case my land is desolate, my people overwhelmed. We cannot cope with you. Gentlemen, consider. Amend your terms. See! I promise that, beautiful as she is, well worthy to be the mother of brave sons, my daughter shall not give herself to any man. She will become a religious.

SINDHIA'S AMBASSADOR. That suits us not. She must marry as we have said.

JAIPUR'S AMBASSADOR. She must fulfil her engagement to us.

SINDHIA'S AMBASSADOR. If not, 'tis war.

[*Exit.*]

JAIPUR'S AMBASSADOR. Ay ! war to the knife.

[*Exit.*]

BHIM SINGH. So, I am undone ! Our world will suffer grievous wrong for the sake of a pretty girl's face.

PRINCESS KRISHNA KUMARI. [*Stepping from behind the latticed alcove.*] Nay ! not so, my father. Lo ! I have heard all, and never through me shall my beloved country be wasted in war. [*She kneels before her father.*] Father ! were I a boy you'd give me leave to fight for Udaipur. Now, since I am but a poor pitiful girl, let me but die for her. What counts my life against a smart or hurt of these poor patient people, who have already stood long years of war and dread adversity ? Lo ! my beauty bids men fight for me ; they'll sheath their swords when it is cold and dead. Brother ! thy knife here in my breast.

[*She bares her bosom.*]

BHIM SINGH. Krishna ! my child. What ! thou wouldst die for us ?

KRISHNA. There is no other way to peace. When I am dead, these princes will not quarrel to possess my corpse.

MOTHER. (*Rushing out.*) No ! no ! this shall not be. Heart's darling ! come. Lo ! I will hide thee safe. No man shall find thee.

KRISHNA. They will find other victims, mother. Let me go where peace dwells ever, where no man can vex my heart or mind. [*Turning to her father.*] Think for a moment, O most revered, most beloved! 'tis one small life against the valued lives of many innocent folks who cling to life — as I do not. Father, let me die!

BHIM SINGH. Her words strike home. These men backed by Maratha force may make my realm a desert.

KRISHNA. Thou seest the truth, my father. I must die. Yet let me die with honour by a noble hand. Brother! the task is thine. Draw out the dagger sacred to our creed of truth and faith, and drive it home. Here, in my heart!

BROTHER. [*Drawing his dagger.*] Noblest of women! Lo! my pride leaps up to join your courage. In long years to come, the Rajput maidens shall sing songs of you and tell how Princess Krishna died. [*He advances to strike the blow but his courage fails him. He throws up his hand and lets the dagger drop, then covers his face with his hands.*] I cannot, oh! I cannot. Sister, forgive me; thou art all too fair for death.

KRISHNA. [*Turning to her mother.*] Mother, I crave from you the last gift that a Rajput mother gives when her daughter's honour is in danger. Mine is sore beset. These princes clamour for me and I will not wed for threats of murder and of pillage. Give me the poison draught that kills as it is drunk. Quick! mother, quick!

MOTHER. Heart's darling! ask me not.

KRISHNA. [*Proudly.*] Lo! I do ask it. Yea, I ask of thee, my mother, to defend the body thou hast borne.

MOTHER. [*Going with tears.*] No mother can refuse that last request.

[*Goes.*]

KRISHNA. [*Smiling.*] Look not so sad, father. And you too, brotherling. Remember how in days long past we women died, braving the fire rather than falling into hands we hated.

BROTHER. But that was different. We men died too, selling each Rajput life for twenty of the *mlechchha*. Now —

KRISHNA. The men are different, and the people crave for peace.

[*Enter* MOTHER *bearing a cup.*]

Thanks, mother! [*Takes it, holds it up.*] To every Rajput soldier of the Sun and to the Sun himself I drink it. [*Drinks: stands for a second. Then turns to her mother.*] Mother! thou hast deceived me. This is not the poisoned draught of death. What matter? I will go and for myself prepare the sweet *kasumba* drink which buys soft sleep that never wakens. Farewell!

[*Goes,* MOTHER *follows weeping.*]

BHIM SINGH. [*Gloomily.*] She is full set on this, and 'tis a way out of our difficulty. And I would rather see her dead than wedded to the minion of that low-bred hound.

BROTHER. And fighting we would have but little chance.

[*Enter* CHAMBERLAIN.]

CHAMBERLAIN. The Chief of Karradur, Sir Sagwant Singh, demands an instant audience. He hath ridden hard.

BHIM SINGH. Let him come in.

[*Enter* SAGWANT SINGH *breathless with haste.*]

SAGWANT SINGH. My lord, my lord! The Princess, does she live?

[BHIM SINGH *and* BROTHER *look at each other and are silent.*]

For I have heard vague rumours that she means to kill herself rather than trust herself to our good swords; and that must never be said. What! shall a Rajput maiden choose the help of death while there remains a man who owns a sword? Old as I am —

[ATTENDANT *and* MOTHER *enter weeping.*]

MOTHER. Lo! she has chosen. On her bed she lies as if asleep. But she will never wake! Ah! woe is me.

SAGWANT SINGH. The Princess, then, is dead?

MOTHER. She will not wake again.

SAGWANT SINGH. [*Turns passionately to* BHIM SINGH *and* KRISHNA'S BROTHER *who cower beneath his wrath. Then unbuckles his sword.*] My ancestors, O King, have served yours for thirty generations, and of blame I dare say nothing; but of this be sure, my sword will ne'er again by drawn for you or yours. I lay it here down in the dust of Kings. Farewell for ever!

[*He lays sword at the foot of the throne and exit.*]

— 27 —

EMPTY EMPIRE.

From the date of Aurangzeb's death the dynasty of the Great Moguls and the Empire founded by great Babur, and handed on intact through greater Akbar and his descendants, Jahangir, Shahjahan, and Aurangzeb, had sunk lower. Still by name the Emperors of India, they ceased to have any power, until in the nineteenth century one Shah Alam, old, miserable, blind, keeping up a ragged royalty in those incomparable palaces at Delhi which neither time nor treachery could touch, placed himself voluntarily under British protection.

He was quite a good man, but helpless — almost imbecile; briefly the degenerate outcome of a long line of men who had forgotten kingship in luxury. He lived for a few years, more or less a prisoner. Then his son reigned as Akbar II., and finally his grandson Bahadur Shah, by his treachery to his protectors, forfeited their support and died in Burma. Thus the Mogul dynasty which began so marvellously came to an end.

DRAMATIS PERSONÆ.

SHAH ALAM, the Mogul, aged, 86, blind, decrepit.
MIRZA AKBAR SHAH, his son aged 57.
MIRZA BAHADUR SHAH, his grandson aged 26.
MIRZA MOGUL, his great-grandson aged 8.
THE DIWAN.
GENERAL LAKE.
HIS A. D. C.
Courtiers.

SCENE.

The Diwan-i-Khas at Delhi. SHAH ALAM *old, blind, seated on ragged cushions under a small tattered tinsel canopy. His sons and nobles all in fine clothes, much worn by age, about him.*

SHAH ALAM. [*Whimpering.*] Will he be as good, think you, as Perron Sahib?

MIRZA AKBAR. Who can say?—but it has to be! The English have beaten the French, and Perron Sahib was a Frenchman.

MIRZA BAHADUR. [*Looking at his little son.*] Ay, if we are to keep the throne of our ancestors for our sons we need protection.

SHAH ALAM. [*Whimpering.*] Protection? Who needs it more than I, the Emperor of all the Indies? Lo! how the wicked have troubled me, poor servant of God, whose life has been spent with saints and sacred books. Hai! Hai! Hai! When I remember—[*Nods his head garrulously.*] How did it begin? I forget. Always the same! Always being asked to sign papers or pay armies, with scarce a pice in the palace to pay for the cook-room. Then when Ghulam Kadir the Rohilla—Hai! Hai!

MIRZA BAHADUR. [*To his little son.*] Mogli, go quick to grand-dad and caress him. That may make him calm.

MIRZA MOGUL. Grand-dad, see I have on my best clothes. Do I not look smart?

SHAH ALAM. [*Fondly.*] Thou lookest what thou art, a prince of Timur's race. But is not the gold upon thy *sarposh* a trifle tarnished? It feels frayed. But I am blind, blind! 'Twas Ghulam Kadir did it.

MIRZA AKBAR. Forget it, father.

SHAH ALAM. Never! He was there down by the scented baths and he asked for hidden treasure and I knew of none. Then, said he, I was of no use and should be blinded; but I begged him to spare the old eyes that for sixty years had grown dim with the daily study of God's Word, and he spared them.

MIRZA BAHADUR. [*Soothingly.*] Yea! yea! He spared them, grand-dad; so let be. The Englishman is coming anon.

SHAH ALAM. [*Unheeding.*] Lo! it is ever before my mind's eye. Akbar, my son! thy groans will kill me. How they tortured you, my sons, my grandsons, to find out where the treasure was hidden—and there was none. I tell you there is none. We have no treasure. "Oh, take my sight, you fiends of the nethermost hell rather than force my eyes to see such scenes, such inhuman cruelties." With that he leapt upon me. I feel the knife in my eyes now. Hai! Hai! Have mercy! Have mercy! [*Weeps.*] [*A bugle sounds.*]

MIRZA AKBAR. Father! for the honour of our House be calm. The English envoy comes. Let him not find the Emperor of India, the descendant of great Babur, in tears.

SHAH ALAM. [*More quietly.*] And wherefore not? Is not a prisoner's life ever full of tears? For how long have I been slave to the Marathas! And now this Englishman—

MIRZA BAHADUR. He will pay better, I think.

SHAH ALAM. [*Drying his eyes.*] Mayhap, mayhap! And we need money sorely. Sure 'tis time, Mirza Akbar, that you went to escort the Englishman hither; and Diwan, go you and see that all is of the strictest etiquette.

DIWAN. As the Most High commands.

[*Bows. Exit after* MIRZA AKBAR.]

SHAH ALAM. Mogli, bring thy club and ball, it may pass the time.

MIRZA MOGUL. Yea, grand-dad.

[*They play. Bugles.*]

[*Enter* GENERAL LAKE *escorted by* MIRZA AKBAR *and* DIWAN *and followed closely by* AIDE-DE-CAMP, *who takes the* GENERAL'S *hat.*]

AIDE-DE-CAMP. Glad to get you here, sir. What a crowd and how strangely they looked at you!

GENERAL LAKE. [*Pompously.*] They were anxious to look at the deliverer of the Sovereign from a state of degradation and bondage.

[*Suitable salutations pass.* GENERAL LAKE *is seated on a chair facing the* MOGUL. *Attar and pan are handed round.*]

GENERAL LAKE. The affair having been previously settled by which the most illustrious monarch Shah Alam, Emperor of all the Indies, does, for due consideration, as mentioned, place himself and his heirs —

MIRZA AKBAR. Huzoor!

GENERAL LAKE.— under the protection of the British Raj, all that is necessary is to affix the signatures to this document. You have it, I think?

AIDE-DE-CAMP. [*Producing deed.*] Yes, sir.

GENERAL LAKE. I will sign first as token of good faith.

[*A writing slab is brought, with pen and ink. He signs.*] Now, Your Majesty.

SHAH ALAM. [*Languidly.*] My seal is here. Take it, my son.

[MIRZA AKBAR *draws the ring from his father's finger, inks it and signs.*]

GENERAL LAKE. So, that is done, and we trust in the future. [*Rises.*]

SHAH ALAM. [*Rises also and looks at his sons helplessly.*] Did you not tell me there was something more?

DIWAN. [*Unctuously.*] Yea! Most Mighty, in consideration of this piece of paper [*Touches deed.*] it is Your Highness's pleasure to bestow on General Lake Sahib Bahadur the titles of "Sword of the State," "Hero of the Land," "Lord of the Age" and "Victorious in War."

COURTIERS. Wah! Wah!

GENERAL LAKE. On behalf of the great Company I serve, I thank Your Majesty for this mark of favour, and I trust in the future.

[*Bows and takes his leave.*]

MIRZA AKBAR. What allowance did they promise in the deed?

DIWAN. It is not mentioned; only that due regard shall be paid to the comfort and convenience of Your Royal Highness.

SHAH ALAM. [*Leaning on his staff.*] I would like to see it once again before I die.

MIRZA BAHADUR. See what, father?

SHAH ALAM. The legend on the wall. [*He looks up.*] Canst read it, Mogli? See it goes round and round; always the same. Read it, child.

MIRZA MOGUL. [*Reading slowly.*] "Agar Firdus-i-Zamin ust, hamin ust, hamin ust, hamin ust."* What does that mean, grand-dad?

[*The old* KING *weeps. The* PRINCES, COURTIERS *bow their heads sadly.*]

* If there be a Paradise upon Earth, it is this, it is this, it is this!

—28—

A BREATHING.

A vast number of the Indian people call the Great Mutiny of 1857 by the name of 'hawa'; that is to say, a wind or breath. A spirit, in other words, swept through the land, driving men hither and thither.

What the real cause of the Mutiny was it is useless to enquire. Volumes have been written about it without further result than to show that nine-tenths of the people of India knew nothing whatever of a purely military mutiny.

What they would have done had they known, it is useless to enquire. Time is better spent in showing what they did.

DRAMATIS PERSONÆ.

FAIZU, the householder.
ADHAM, his son.
JEWANI, his wife.
FATIMA, his daughter-in-law.
NANNI, his old mother.
IMAM, his brother, an old servant of the Sahib-log.

SCENE.

The village hut of a Ranghar family in the Rohtak district. It is night.

The householder, an old man, is eating his supper. His son, a man of middle age, has just come in and is smoking his chillum. A very old woman squats by the fire stirring a pot of milk. A young woman sits in a corner veiled. The house-mother is bustling about over the supper.

FAIZU. When I was watering the fields to-day I saw a great body of horsemen on the horizon. I wonder who they were!

JEWANI. The Toorks, mayhap. Nanni is always talking of them. She says she saw some when she was gathering radishes at the well the other day, but they had white faces like the Sahibs. She hid herself for fear. [*Bawling.*] Didn't you, Nanni?

NANNI. [*Stirring the milk.*] Ay! ay! The Toork goes and he comes, but they should be all dead by now. The last came just after I was born. My mother caught me up and fled to the wilderness. And her *nanni* told tales. Ay! ay! [*Falls to singing.*] "The Toork! the Toork! he will find you."

ADHAM. [*Bawling.*] Peace, grandam. I know not, father, who they might be, but at the market to-day, folks were saying there was a breath in the land.

FATIMA. [*Suddenly breaking in, her voice full of tears.*] What care I now that the only breath I cared for has ceased. Hai! Hai! my baby, my little baby, my little son.

JEWANI. Peace! peace! daughter-in-law. Disturb not the men with thy grief. Lo! I wept full sore when my firstling went; but God sent another and I was comforted.

NANNI. [*To herself.*] Ay! ay! He sends the children sure enough: they be His children ever.

FAIZU. What were they saying at the market. Adham?

ADHAM. Nothing for certain, father, though some said there was to be a new master and that the Sahibs were to be turned out.

FAIZU. Allah! Wherefore? Did not the *burra* Sahib give justice in my case and I paid naught for it? What more does one want in a law-court?

ADHAM. And one—he was a stranger—said the Sahibs made their servants Christians by force.

FAIZU. That is a lie. Thine uncle Imam hath served the Sahib-log for fifty years, and if ever there was a pious one 'tis he. [*Speaking emphatically.*] Yea, Imam Khan is a saint and a pilgrim too.

NANNI. Imam Khan? Ay! he is my eldest born, a goodly godly lad. Faizu, why does he not come home and till the land like his fathers?

FAIZU. [*Bawling.*] He hath left the land to my care, mother. Mind you he hath no kind of his own.

NANNI. Ay! ay! he is a saint. He broke his heart when Zuleika and her babe died. Imam, my little lad! I should like to see him again.

FATIMA. [*Bawling.*] Was the child old when it died, Nanni?

NANNI. As thine child, suckling. Nay weep not! If thou art patient God will send another.

FAIZU. Yea! yea! I should like to see Imam again. We were right fond of each other as boys; but see you he grew restless and went to serve the *Sirkar.* And now that he has grown old, he serves the *Sirkar* still but not in the regiment. So it is a lie that they force people to be Christians. Imam knows the Holy Book by heart.

[*Someone tries the door.*]

ADHAM. Hist! there is someone at the door. Retire, women, till I see who 'tis.

[*The two women huddle into a corner. Old* NANNI *remains stirring the milk.* ADHAM *opens the door. An old man spent and blood-stained, carrying a bundle, staggers in and goes to the fire.*]

[*Ere he reaches it he stumbles, half falls, and the bundle he carries falls on* NANNI'S *lap. The man sits back on his knees face to face with* NANNI. *She peers at him, then cries.*]

NANNI. Imam! Imam! my son, my little son. See he is blood-stained. See to him, Jewani. I cannot rise.

IMAM. [*Faintly.*] Nay! nay! It is naught. I am but out-wearied. A drink of water for Heaven's sake.

FAIZU. [*Loudly.*] Quick! Give him water.

[NANNI, *swift as thought, lifts off the milkpot, pours some into a lotah and gives it him.*]

NANNI. [*Tenderly.*] As in the old days, O my son! Now art thou safe at home with Ammajan.

[IMAM *drinks, sets down the lotah with a deep sigh of content.*]

IMAM. Yea! God and his Propnet be praised. We are safe.

FAIZU But Imam, tell us what —

IMAM. God knows what! It came in a moment like a breath from Hell, maddening all. It was the hour of prayer. Then in a second the sepoys were shooting.

They killed the Colonel Sahib—but it was not my Colonel Sahib: he found freedom years ago; but my Captain Sahib was his son and I served him and the *baba*; for lo! the little *mem-sahib* died when it was born. So as the Captain Sahib lay wounded to death there was content in his eyes as he said, "There is only the child, Imam, only the child. Save him!" So I ran like a hare, and gave it a pellet of the dream-compeller to stop its cries. [*A pause.*]

ADHAM. And then?

IMAM. I hid in the cane-brakes by day and gave the babe the sugar-water to drink, and at night I ran on and on and on. I thought—[*His voice grows a little weak.*] of finding you my mother. Then the child—[*He leans forward and undoes the bundle a little so that no one but* NANNI *can see.*] Lo! he sleeps well, the *chhota* Sahib.

NANNI. [*Arms close round the bundle in a moment, murmuring.* A child! a little child!

[*The other women crowd round and peer.*]

JEWANI. Lo! how white it is.

FATIMA. Its hair is as gold.

IMAM. Take care of it, mother, so shall I not have eaten of my master's salt in vain.

NANNI. [*Rises tall and upstanding and puts the bundle into* FATIMA's *arms.*] Did I not tell thee, child, God would send another? Nourish this one as thine own.

FAIZU and ADHAM. But the neighbours?

[*The three women laugh.*]

JEWANI. [*With a superior air.*] Bullah! Hast never heard of dye stuffs? Go quick, Adham, to the village shop and buy a pennyworth.

—29—

THE EMPIRE.

In 1911, for the first time in the History of India, an Emperor of all the India, not only of a part of it, sate on the throne of the Empire in Delhi. Asoka, Akbar, Chandragupta, even the half mythical King of Kings of whom we catch faint glimpses in the dark ages of Indian History, never held the sceptre over so large a portion of the earth as does George V., Kaiser-i-Hind. After the mistaken Mutiny of 1857 Queen Victoria abolished the old East India Company and undertook the government of India herself. In 1872 she proclaimed herself Empress of India, but it was left to her grandson George V. to travel out from England and once more give his Indian subjects the pleasure and privilege of seeing their own Emperor seated on the throne where so many Emperors have sate. Time brings many changes, but though the form is altered the spirit remains the same, for it is the spirit of slaves that dies, the spirit of kings lives for ever. So the wisdom of Asoka and the wisdom of Akbar spoke in the words of the great Emperor who sate on the throne on that fateful day of the great Imperial Durbar.

And that wisdom is this. That true Government can only exist through justice and charity, truth and purity, kindness and goodness.

DRAMATIS PERSONÆ.

MASTERJI.

GUNGA, a Hindu schoolboy, Bunya caste.

KRISHNA, a Hindu schoolboy, Brahman caste.

FATTEH, } Mahomedan schoolboys.
FAIZU, }

BUDDHA, a very old Hindu.

ANAND, a saintly old Hindu (blind).

IMAM, } Mahomedan village elders.
HUSSAIN, }

SCENE.

The plain outside Delhi. A village cart drawn up behind the line of spectators. It is crowded with village schoolboys. At the foot of it a group of men.

ANAND. Nay! Masterji, thou must go up. We old ones have seen enough in our time. As for me I am blind, so thy telling shall be my eyes.

CHORUS OF BOYS. Yea! Masterji, come up. We shall not understand without you.

MASTERJI. So be it, boys. [*Climbs up and stands in middle of the cart. He looks about.*] There is nothing yet but soldiers, soldiers everywhere. I cannot compute how many there be.

HUSSAIN. [*From below.*] 'Tis not numbers that count, Masterji. The Northerners were but 20,000 at Paniput, yet —

BUDDHA. Talk not of Paniput, my son. There have been too many battles there to know which be which.

MASTERJI. True, O Babaji! It is computed that two million men be buried beneath the sand of that desolate plain.

GUNGA. [*Fearfully.*] Is it true, Masterji, that on moonlight nights you can hear their bones fighting still beneath the sand?

MASTERJI. Such talk is foolishness.

BUDDHA. Yet have I heard it when I was young, and so —

ANAND. [*Interfering.*] Yet, does it matter now how many be dead? For see you as great Asoka wrote: "Conquest by the sword is not worthy the name of conquest."

MASTERJI. True, most true, old friend! And this new Empire of ours stands, as Asoka had it, by justice and charity, truth and purity, kindness and goodness. Come boys, tell me wherein the greatness of our Empire lies. Give us for and against as in fair argument.

KRISHNA. There were no schools in old time.

MASTERJI. Ho! ho! Go up one. Is that for or against?

[BOYS *laugh; some say,* "For," *some* "Against."]

Lo! I must ask the elders first. What think you, Babaji? Are we worse or better?

BUDDHA. 'Tis better for old men, for see you there is peace.

ANAṆD. And it is better for devotion, for see you, all have freedom.

IMAM. Ay, friend, I am with you there. It is the house of protection.

HUSSAIN. And it is better for comfort. See you, there be postmen and railway trains and telegrams and — and —

GUNGA. And matches, Babaji!

FAIZU. And middle schools!!

KRISHNA. And masters!!!

[*A roar of laughter.*]

MASTERJI. Now, boys, steady! till I make you understand. On those red rocks before us the English stood to wage a battle for freedom for the people. Babaji, you remember when General Lake Sahib came to give protection to the Badshah Shah Alam. How was it then?

BUDDHA. [*Shaking his head.*] Ay! ay! I was there. It was a sorry sight, and the land so bested with Marathas that there was no room for peaceable folk.

MASTERJI. And you, Anand?

ANAND. [*Shaking his head.*] It is past, Masterji. What need for praise or blame?

MASTERJI. And you, Imam?

IMAM. [*Sighing.*] It would not have been so bad could one but have had justice; but each man's hand was in his neighbour's pocket.

HUSSAIN. [*Laughing.*] To find nothing! No, Masterji, there is more prosperity now-a-days and it will go on increasing. We tillers of the soil have enough four-anna bits to put them on our cart wheels.

FAIZU. And to give me one for sweets.

[*Roars of laughter.*]

MASTERJI. Silence! Yes, the fight was for freedom, to keep us from falling back into the tyranny of the past.

[*A sudden loud roar of a gun.*]

[*Holding up his hand.*] Listen! that is the first gun of the Imperial salute. Cheer! boys, cheer! See there comes the Emperor! — in the far far distance that cloud of dust.

BOYS. [*Crowd round.*] Where, Masterji? Oh, yes! he is coming. Listen to the roar of the guns. Ah! ah! ah!

BUDDHA. Tell us when he passes, Masterji, that we may *durshan* as well as we can.

[*The* ELDERS *rise up in a row and stand eager.*]

BOYS. Look! look!

GUNGA. That's he! See his crown!

KRISHNA. Oh! look the orb in his hand!

FAIZU. And the sceptre!

FUTTEH. He is just like the pictures.

[*They break into wild huzzas.*]

MASTERJI. Now! now! ye elders of the village.

[*The* OLD MEN *all salaam and join in, as best they can,* "God Save Our Gracious King," *which the* MASTER *starts.*]